THE GREAT BOOK OF
DENVER SPORTS LISTS

THE GREAT BOOK OF DENVER

SPORTS LISTS

BY JOE WILLIAMS AND IRV BROWN

RUNNING PRESS
PHILADELPHIA · LONDON

9 8 7 6 5 4 3 2 1

Digit on the right indicates the number of this printing

Library of Congress Control Number: 2008926941

ISBN 978-0-7624-3355-1

Cover and Interior Designed by Matthew Goodman
Edited by Lisa Jones, Verbal Construction

Running Press Book Publishers
2300 Chestnut Street
Philadelphia, PA 19103-4371

Visit us on the web!
www.runningpress.com

Dedication

This book is dedicated to our wives with love: Pat Brown and Charlotte Williams.

Acknowledgments

We'd like to thank Jeanine DeFrancesco for her hard work and dedication. We couldn't have done it without you, Jeanine. Many thanks to Tim Spence, Dan Jacobs, Jim Armstrong and Bob Call—you have our admiration and gratitude. Also, thanks to Greg Jones at Running Press and Lisa Jones (no relation) at Verbal Construction for their help down the homestretch.

CONTENTS

Introduction 11

Top Ten Finest Gentlemen in Colorado Sports 12

Worst Decisions in Denver Sports 14

Top Opponents (by Joel Quenneville) 16

Best Broncos Game Ever 17

Most Devastating Broncos Losses 19

What's In A Name? 21

Five Best Coaching Performances in Nuggets History (by Andrew Feinstein) 23

Five Worst Coaching Performances in Nuggets History (by Andrew Feinstein) 24

Most Memorable Baseball Moments (by John Hickenlooper) 25

Key Events in Early Broncos History (by Dave Kopel) 27

Bobby Unser is Driven 29

King of the Mountain (by Bobby Unser) 30

Best Sports Movies (by Michael Booth) 31

Our Top Ten Sports Movies 33

Most Memorable Athlete Performances in Movies (by Michael Booth) 35

Irv's Top Movies About Coaching and Motivation 36

Joe's Five Favorite College Football Films 37

Best Sports Movies According to Our Listeners 38

Colorado's Best Women Athletes (by Dorothy Mauk) 39

Top Five Early Rockies 44

The First Rockies Played Hockey (by Terry Frei) 46

Three Things You Probably Didn't Know About the Broncos
    (by Jim Saccomano) 47

Broncos Draft Misses and Hits (by Joe Williams) 48

First Round Picks that Didn't Stick 50

Broncos Trivia Tutorial #1 51

Calling It Like I See It (by Jim Evans) 53

Guys Who Don't Get Enough Credit 56

Our Favorite Avs 58

My Top Ten Denver Sports Highlights (by Adam Clayton-Holland) 59

Most Astonishing Series of One Game Performances by Denver Pros 62

Highlights Beyond the Orange and Blue 64

Five Nuggets for All Time (by Nick Sclafani) 66

Long-Gone Colorado Teams 68

Top Colorado Pitchers 70

Five Toughest Hitters (by Goose Gossage) 71

Five Favorite Pitchers (by Bus Campbell) 72

Best All Around Baseball Players (by Tony DeMarco) 73

Bauldie Moschetti and the Boulder Collegians 74

Our Favorite Players and Memories at Merchants Park 76

Our Favorite Billy Martin Quotes 78

Top Five MLB Scouts (by Dick Balderson) 79

Ten Best Pioneer Baseball Players (by Jack Rose) 80

Our All-Time Top 50 Pros 81

Our Listeners List the Best Players Ever 86

Mecklenburg Never Took a Play Off 88

Toughest Guys Ever to Play Football in Colorado 89

Toughest Wideouts to Cover (by Louis Wright) 90

In Rod We Trust 91

Five Toughest NHL Players (by Brett Clark) 92

Five Toughest Centers (by Bill Hanzlik) 93

Homegrown Baseball Pros 94

Five Favorite Interviewees (by Woody Paige) 96

Dan's Best Sportswriters 97

Best Three-Point Shooters 98

Broncos Trivia Tutorial #2 99

Five Tough Offensive Linemen (by Alfred Williams) 101

Most Memorable Kicks (by David Treadwell) 102

From Player to Coach 103

Great Colorado Golfers 105

Irv Picks the Best Junior Golfers (by Irv Brown) 106

Best Colorado Golf Courses (by John Edwards) 108

Irv's Golf Course Picks 112

Best Public Golf Courses 113

What We'll Miss About The International 114

Best Denver Boxers (by Dave Sidwell) 115

Irv's Top Ten College Football Games 118

Joe's Top Bowl Games (by Joe Williams)120

Best College Football Coaches Ever 121

My Favorite Buffs (by Irv Brown) 122

Notable Buffaloes (by Bill McCartney) 125

Five Downs Not Four 126

Top College Football Teams (by Pat Forde) 127

A Nod to the Buckeyes (by Tom Kensler) 128

Amazing Airforce Athletes (Troy Garnhart) 129

DU Football Memories 131

Irv's Favorite UNC Bears 132

Irv's Favorite Rams (by Irv Brown) 134

Hat Tip to the School of Mines 136

Irv's Top College Basketball Players in Colorado 137

Best Wyoming Cowboys (by Ryan Thornburn) 140

The Best Game Ever (by Charlie Brown) 142

Broncos Trivia Tutorial #3 143

Top Preps on CET (by Brian Roth) 145

Swimming With Lions (by Maurice "Stringy" Ervin) 147

Top Women's Volleyball Players (by Lo Hunter) 148

Irv's 100 Best Ever High School Players in the Metro Area 149

Things You Might Not Know About Irv (by Joe Williams) 157

Favorite Final Fours 158

Explosive Basketball Coaches 159

Irv's Secrets for Success in Sports (by Irv Brown) 160

Zebras from Denver 161

Notable Broncos Assistants 162

Local Team Nicknames 163

Great Names and Nicknames in Colorado Sports 164

Sportscasters We'll Never Forget 166

Best Trivia Shows on TV (by Tom Green) 168

A Dozen Great Interviews (by Mark McIntosh) 169

Golden Voices (by Jim Conrad) 170

Favorite Soccer Moments (by Vic Lombardi) 171

An Anchor picks His Top News Stories (by Jim Benemann) 172

Talking Pros 173

Sports Media Gone But Not Forgotten (by Bob Martin) 174

Players Who Made Me an Avalanche Fan (by Aaron D'Albey) 175

Lore to Store 177

Hoop Dreams at the Auditorium Arena 179

Top Basketball Players from Back in the Day (by Vince Boryla) 181

Colorado Women Hoops Stars (by Ceal Barry) 182

The Denver Viners (by Irv Brown) 183

Best Basketball Pros (by Jeff Bzdelik) 184

Best Big Guys in Basketball (Ervin Johnson) 185

Three Basketball Dream Teams 186

Bad Pickaxe Picks (by Chris Dempsey) 188

Irv Picks The Best College Basketball Coaches Ever in Colorado 189

It Spells Trouble 190

Johnsons We're Glad to See 192

Colorado's Best Track Competitions (by John Hancock) 193

Great Colorado Runners (by John Meyer) 195

Denver Makes a Run for It 196

Five Places to Run 197

More Great Colorado Runners (by John Meyer) 198

A Couple of Characters (by Irv Brown) 199

Athletes from Colorado Springs (by Mike Spence) 200

A Selection of Avalanche Highlights (by Terry Frei) 201

Irv Picks the Best Buffs Who Went Pro 206

Best Denver Pro Players Not Born in the USA 207

Greatest Duos in Colorado Sports 208

How the Drive Went Down 210

Jim "Tank" Turner 211

Orange Crush Ain't Sodypop 212

Best Broncos by the Numbers 214

Sports Legends from Z to A 221

Our Namedropping List 224

Nastiest Defense Linemen (by Babe Parilli) 227

Worst Time Ever for Denver Sports 228

Irv Remembers When Softball Was King 229

The Comeback Kid 230

Introduction: What It Was Was a Book of Lists

Look, we're not sportswriters. We're sports talkers. We're fans who love to jaw with other fans about sports. We love athletes who play their hearts out. We love a hard-fought contest, a good meal and an appropriate beverage to wash it down.

Denver has a wealth of outstanding sportswriters. We ain't them. Our on-air colleague Jim Armstrong—he's one of them. He's an award-winning columnist. There's no way we can give you the same level of analytical, informed, well-crafted commentary that a pro like Jim can deliver.

So we offer you a book of lists.

Lists are short and sweet and meant to get you talking. Lists are a way to swap trivia, jog memories and hash out opinions. Listing is a group activity. The more the merrier.

We're thankful to our many friends who contributed lists to this book. They add class and substance. We need all we can get.

This is a book for fans. Sure, all fans mouth off and take shots at players, coaches or owners every now and then. But it's all about love of the game. Denver is a town of fans, not a town of haters.

Denver fans stood by their teams and cheered for decades back when no one was bringing home championship titles. Sometimes we had to grit our teeth and rise above our disappointment. No matter what, Denver fans don't desert their teams. We stick even when our teams stink. That's the Denver fan ethic.

Now that some of our teams have championship victories under their belts, it's easy to see why Denver fans might get a little spoiled and fussy. There's more glitz and glamor now, more money, higher expectations, plus new stadiums and arenas. Denver is a big-time sports town. That's worth celebrating. That's partly what this book is about.

Still, there has to be a place for nostalgia, a place to celebrate forgotten heroes and unsung contributions to Colorado sports. We hope you'll find some of that in this book, too.

Things change. Players get traded. Records get broken. Coaches leave. When we started writing this book, we had no hope of seeing Peter Forsberg in an Avs sweater ever again. This book is not meant to be definitive. As things change, please write your own revisions in the margins.

Also, we know that some of you are gonna read this on the can. We're thinking of you. We've varied the length of our lists so you'll be able to find one that suits your needs.

If nothing else, this book will be among the very best coasters you will ever own. We like to think that our literary effort will prevent your beer bottle from leaving a ring on a table somewhere, somehow. We can dream.

Thanks for reading.
Irv & Joe

To pick only ten of the finest gentlemen in Colorado sports is a daunting task. Hundreds of fellows are worthy of esteem, including stars such as Haven Moses, Floyd Little and Jason Elam. Many great guys have worked behind the scenes—most people wouldn't recognize their names. We had to narrow it down. We polled our listeners. We discussed and deliberated. We're comfortable with our choices.

10. Ben Martin.

The Father of Air Force football, Ben was head coach from 1958 to 1977. Ben was an incredible motivator who got a young program going. He'd take on all the big boys. He had great people skills. Our listeners picked Randy Gradishar, the finest linebacker to ever wear the orange and blue. He spent 10 seasons with the Broncos and was an integral part of the famous Orange Crush defense. He has been a Colorado Sports Hall of Famer since 1987. It's frustrating that he isn't in the Hall of Fame in Canton.

9. John Lynch.

The Bronco safety brings it every play and is accessible in the community. Nine-time Pro Bowl selection. Our listeners picked Karl Mecklenburg, a terrific linebacker who still makes many public appearances. Mecklenburg is a Colorado Sports Hall of Famer who created a charitable foundation for children's education.

8. Joe Sakic.

Not only is Sakic the Avs all-time top goal scorer, he and his wife are active in the community. He hosts a charity golf tournament to help feed the poor. Our listeners picked former Nugget Dikembe Mutombo, a true humanitarian helping to improve living conditions in the Democratic Republic of Congo. Mutombo was the leader when number-eight-seed Denver beat number-one Seattle. He was perhaps the best shot-blocker ever in the NBA, and very popular with the fans in Denver.

7. Sonny Lubick.

He turned CSU's football program around when it was a graveyard. In fifteen seasons as head coach, he won more than 100 games and took his team to nine bowl games. You would be hard pressed to find anyone to say a bad word about Sonny. Our listeners picked Matt Holliday. Matt has been with the Rockies only a short time but the fans adore him. In two years he could have a contract worth $100 million.

6. Sam Suplizio.

He was a beloved civic leader and successful businessman. In the 1950s, a broken wrist derailed his career with the Yankees. He coached the Brewers in the 1982 World Series. He served on both the Colorado Baseball Commission and the Denver Football Commission, and was instrumental in the development of the Rockies. What he did for Grand Junction was amazing. He was a great baseball man and a better person. Our listeners picked Joe Sakic.

5. Bill McCartney.

He coached the University of Colorado Buffalos to a national championship victory in 1990. He has to be the greatest motivator ever. He started Promise Keepers, a Christian organization for men. Our listeners picked Chopper Travaglini. The Denver Nugget trainer was a flesh-and-blood Damon Runyon character. People adored him. There's a Denver street named after Chopper. The Pepsi Center, home of the Nuggets, Avalanche and other teams, is located at 1000 Chopper Circle.

4. John Elway.

The pro football Hall of Famer never turned down a kid asking for an autograph. The most visible person in the state—and he hasn't suited up in years. Our listeners picked Sonny Lubick.

3. Doug Moe.

Moe was the most winning coach in Denver Nuggets history. Doug never took himself too seriously. He always had the time of day for everybody. Our listeners picked LaPhonso Ellis. You never heard a bad word about the guy from Notre Dame. Never had a bad day as a Denver Nugget.

2. Bob Howsam.

Denver's Mr. Baseball. He became the owner of the Denver Bears in the late 1940s. Along with his father and brother, he built Bears Stadium, which became Mile High. Bob was amazing for Denver. He was a founder and principle owner of the Broncos. He sold the team to the Phipps brothers in 1964. He was the GM for the St. Louis Cardinals in 1964 when they won the World Series. He was also the architect of the Big Red Machine in Cincinnati. Our listeners picked John Lynch.

1. Bill Daniels.

A Colorado native, he was a Golden Gloves boxer and Navy man who made a fortune, lost a fortune, and made a fortune. People call him the "father of cable television" because he helped to finance the phenomenal growth of that industry. Daniels co-owned the Los Angeles Lakers and the ABA Utah Stars. A remarkably generous philanthropist, he endowed the University of Denver School of Business, which was renamed for him, and convinced the school to emphasize the teaching of business ethics. He never had a bad word for anyone. Supportive of Ron Lyle, he helped keep the Denver baseball dream alive. What Bill Daniels did for local charities is mind-boggling. He donated his mansion, Cableland, to the City of Denver. Our listeners picked John Elway.

Not just a bad play call here and there. No, we're talking serious errors in judgment. Some were obvious mistakes from the outset. Some became disastrous in retrospect.

8. Lou Saban fires Floyd Little.

On the field, during a game against the Bills. It was symptomatic of Lou's troubled tenure with the Broncos. As the now-legendary story goes, Little refused to be fired. He took the field, caught a pass and scored a heroic touchdown as Sabin fumed on the sidelines.

7. Hearts set on Steppe.

In 1985 the Denver Nuggets had the 19th pick overall in the draft. For one month they kept touting Brooke Steppe from Georgia Tech as their pick. Kansas City had the 18th pick, and they took Steppe. The Nuggets were shocked and didn't have another pick. They called Larry Brown who suggested Rob Williams from Houston. He became a Nugget.

6. Dale Carter.

In 1999 Dale Carter came here from Kansas City. The Broncos paid the cornerback who had played at Tennessee a lot of money. He had a lot of issues off the field. Substance abuse and such. He lasted one year.

5. Ted Gregory.

The Broncos drafted nose tackle Ted Gregory from Syracuse in 1985 in the first round 26th overall. He couldn't play. It was a big mistake. They don't even list him in the Press Guide under the All Time Roster list. Dan Reeves met him for the first time and was shocked to see he was taller than Gregory. Gregory didn't last a year. He became a stockbroker.

4. Mike Lansing.

In 1998, the Rockies gave Mike Lansing a big contract as a free agent. He never lived up to the expectations. He was an All-Star in Montreal. Not so in Denver.

3. Neagle and Hampton.

In 2001 the Rockies gave pitchers Mike Hampton and Denny Neagle millions of dollars. It strangled the club financially for years. Neagle was a fly ball pitcher who never really did it. He suffered elbow and shoulder injuries. The Rockies terminated Neagle's contract after he was busted with a prostitute, and then was busted for driving while impaired a few days later. Hampton was successful early but when they traded his catcher, Brett Mayne, he was ineffective.

2. Firing Doug Moe.

Comsat owned the Nuggets. Robert Wissler was the president and he fired popular Doug Moe who had won 432 games. At the press conference, Moe had to go to the microphone and fire himself. No one from management would do it. Doug's wife, "Big Jane," went to the mic and asked, "Where do we pick up the checks?"

1. Firing Red Miller.

In 1980 Edgar Kaiser bought the Denver Broncos. He didn't know who the coach was. Red Miller had record of 40-22. He took the team to the playoffs three out of four years, and had one trip to the Super Bowl to his credit. Kaiser fired Red who later sued and won an age discrimination suit.

Note: Former Colorado Avalanche Head Coach Joel Quenneville's history in Colorado spans three decades as a player, assistant coach and Head Coach. He roamed the blue line for the NHL's pre-Avalanche Colorado Rockies from 1980-82. He returned to Colorado as an assistant coach with the Avalanche during its inaugural 1995-96 Stanley Cup season. He coached the St. Louis Blues but returned to Colorado in 2004 as the club's Head Coach. The Avs let him go after the team fell to Detroit in the second round of the playoffs in 2008. That seemed like a bum decision to us. Joel provides a list of the top five players he skated against during his days roaming the blue line in the NHL.

5. Dennis Potvin.
He did everything right. Made all the plays.

4. Ray Bourque.
Always on the ice. Made things happen. He was tough to face.

3. Bryan Trottier.
A fierce competitor.

2. Mario Lemieux.
Virtually unstoppable when he had the puck.

1. Wayne Gretzky.
He did things nobody else could do.

Best Broncos Games Ever

Every game is a big event for Denver Broncos fans. This town lives and dies with the team—at least for the span of the game and well into the following workweek. Here are ten games that most Denver fans remember vividly, with the possible exception of number 3. That might've been before your time. Great games, all.

10. 1989 AFC Divisional Playoff game.

Denver 24, Pittsburgh 23. The crowd was the loudest we've ever heard at Mile High. The Broncos trailed until 2.27 seconds left in the game. Trying to rally his team for a game winning field goal, Steelers QB (and future Bronco back-up QB) Bubby Brister fumbled on his own 20. Did we mention that the crowd was the loud? Our ears are still ringing.

9. 1997 AFC Wild Card game.

Hah. Revenge for 1996. In 1996, the Broncos were top seed in the AFC with a record of 13-3. But the Jags came to Mile High and won in an upset, 30-27. In the 1997 AFC Wild Card game, Denver ran the Jaguars out of town, trouncing them 42-17. The Broncos scored in each of the first three possessions. Terrell Davis rushed for 184 yards and had two touchdowns. Five out of our six touchdowns came on run plays.

8. 1998 AFC Divisional Playoff game.

Denver 38, Miami 3. The game marked five straight consecutive post-season wins. John Elway vs. Dan Marino. John threw for 182 yards and one touchdown. Marino for 243 yards. Terrell Davis averaged nine yards per carry.

7. 1989 AFC Championship game.

Denver 37, Cleveland 21. Brown's coach Marty Schottenheimer had to be talking to himself. No luck vs. Denver. Sammy Winder had two TDs.

6. 1997 AFC Championship game.

Denver 24, Pittsburgh 21. At Three Rivers Stadium, Elway had clutch TD passes to Howard Griffith and Ed McCaffrey. Denver fans were in the grip of Super Bowl fever.

5. 1987 AFC Championship game.

Denver won 38-33 over Cleveland. QBs John Elway and Bernie Kosar, respectively, were superb in front of 79,993 fans at Mile High Stadium. It came down to Jerome Castillo stripping the ball from Ernest Byner at the three-yard line with 1.12 seconds left on the clock.

4. 1986 AFC Championship.

Denver beat Cleveland 23-20 in overtime. "The Drive" started on the two-yard line. Keith Bishop said, "We got 'em right where we want 'em." John Elway led a 98-yard drive that culminated with an Elway-to-Mark-Jackson TD pass with 37 seconds left in regulation. Barefoot Rich Karlis kicked the point after to tie. Then he kicked a shoeless field goal in overtime to win it, sending the Broncos to Super Bowl XXII to face the Redskins. Notice that Super Bowl XXII is not one of the games on this list.

3. Super Bowl XII.

Denver 10, Dallas 27. Wait—how can a stinging defeat be ranked as the number-three best game in Broncos history? Because Denver will never equal the Broncomania of 1977, the team's first Super Bowl year. Forget the ultimate loss to Dallas in New Orleans. Broncos Head Coach Robert "Red" Miller owned the town. Running back Jon Keyworth recorded the song, "Make Those Miracles Happen." Miracles seemed possible. People painted their cars orange in honor of the Orange Crush defense. The town went crazy for the Broncos. It was unbeatable.

2. Super Bowl XXXIII.

Denver 34, Atlanta Falcons 19. Denver, coached by Mike Shanahan, played the team of former Broncos coach Dan Reeves for the 1998 championship. Dan and John Elway weren't too friendly—bad history from Reeves' days in Denver. Elway was the game's MVP with 18 of 29 passes completed and 336 yards—the most in Super Bowl history. After the game, Broncos Owner Pat Bowlen raised the Lombardi trophy and said "This one's for John." Indeed.

1. Super Bowl XXXII.

Broncos 31, Packers 24. In 1997, the Broncos were a 12-point underdog to Brett Favre and Green Bay. Terrell Davis tore up the pack with 157 yards on 30 carries and was named the MVP. Tyrone "Chicken" Braxton had a key pick on a Favre pass. Jason Elam had a 51-yard field goal—the second longest in Super Bowl history.

Most Devastating Broncos Losses

Here we catalog the most soul-crushing defeats. You might want to skip this list. You probably already know it by heart.

11. 2005 AFC Championship Game.
January 22, 2006. Pittsburgh Steelers 34, Broncos 17. Broncos were favored by three. They swallowed the apple whole as the Steelers denied the Broncos a sixth Super Bowl appearance.

10. 1991 AFC Championship Game.
Buffalo 10, Denver 7. The Broncos defense was brilliant, holding Jim Kelly and Thurman Thomas in check. But the Broncos offense sputtered.

9. 1993 AFC Wild Card.
LA Raiders 42, Denver 24. Jeff Hostetler threw for three touchdowns. John Elway matched him with three. The Raiders were the better team in the second half.

8. Super Bowl XII.
Dallas 27, Denver 10. The Cowboys were favored and ended the Broncos 1977 dream season. The clincher was when Roger Staubach pitched the ball to Robert Newhouse who completed a pass to Golden Richards for 29 yards and a touchdown.

7. Super Bowl XXI.
January 25, 1987. New York Giants 39, Denver 20. A close game was broken open by 24 unanswered points. Phil Simms set more Super Bowl passing records as the Broncos offense disappeared in the second half. Simms got a trip to Disneyland, completed 22 of 25 passes, three touchdowns.

6. 2004 AFC Wild Card.
Indianapolis 49; Denver 24. That man Peyton threw for 458 yards with four touchdowns. Reggie Wayne had two of them.

5. 2003 AFC Wild Card Game.
Indianapolis 41, Denver 10. You got a sick feeling when Peyton Manning led the Colts on a 70-yard touchdown drive to open the game. It was over at halftime. The Colts led 31-3. Manning threw five touchdown passes.

4. 2000 AFC Wild Card Game.
Baltimore 23, Denver 3. Ray Lewis was the leader of the defense that held the Broncos to 177 yards. The club's third lowest output in 28 post-season games.

3. Super Bowl XXII.
January 31, 1988. Washington 42, Denver 10. This was supposed to be easy. The Broncos were favored by three points and had an early 10-point lead. Skins finally settled on Doug Williams at quarterback. He outplayed John Elway. Broncos offense disappeared. Timmy Smith had a career day—204 yards rushing and two touchdowns. Doug Williams threw four touchdowns in the game.

2. 1996 AFC Playoff Game.

January 4, 1997. Jacksonville 30, Denver 27. The Broncos were a 12-point favorite. Lefty Mark Brunell was brilliant. His third down pass to Jimmy Smith for a touchdown was the dagger. It was the second biggest upset in NFL postseason history. Shannon Sharpe said that losing the game set the franchise back ten years.

1. Super Bowl XXIV.

January 28, 1990. San Francisco 55, Denver 10. The Broncos, a ten-point underdog, were blown out by possibly the greatest offensive team in NFL history. Joe Montana threw five touchdown passes—three to Jerry Rice. He had a baseball cap on early and Steve Young played quarterback. They ended up naming a state after Montana. The Broncos were objects of derision for the next seven years on late night TV.

As Denver teams have evolved over the years, so have team names. Here's a look back at the name game.

Basketball

5. AAU Nuggets.
In the 1930s and 40s, Denver's local amateur team was called the Nuggets. Those Nuggets won a national Amateur Athletic Union title in 1939.

4. Short-lived Nuggets.
A pro team called the Denver Nuggets played losing basketball from 1948-50. They had few fans and didn't last long.

3. Keep on truckin'.
The D-C Truckers (backed by the Denver-Chicago Trucking Company) were a popular amateur team in the 1950s and 60s.

2. Larks become Rockets.
Denver's ABA franchise in 1967 was originally called the Denver Larks. Bill Ringsby, who made his fortune in trucking, bought control of the team. His trucks were known as Ringsby Rockets, and the basketball team was christened the Denver Rockets.

1. Rockets become Nuggets.
Under new ownership in 1974, the Denver Rockets were re-named the Denver Nuggets. The team was absorbed into the NBA in 1977.

Hockey

3. Spurs.
A minor-league hockey team called the Denver Spurs played briefly in the Mile High City before moving to Canada in the 1975-76 season.

2. Scouts become Rockies become Devils.
In 1976, the NHL Kansas City Scouts moved to Denver and were re-christened the Colorado Rockies. They moved east in 1982 to become the New Jersey Devils.

1. Nordiques become Avs.
In 1995, owners of the NHL Quebec Nordiques relocated the franchise to Denver. The name "Rocky Mountain Avalanche" was suggested. "Denver Avalanche" had been the name of a pro soccer team from 1980-82. The owners ultimately settled on the Colorado Avalanche.

Baseball

4. Bronchos with an "H."
In the early 1920s, a semi-pro team called the Denver Bronchos emerged and quickly disappeared. Broncho is the old-skool spelling of bronco, an unbroken mustang.

3. Bears.
A minor-league team called the Bears or the Grizzlies played off and on in Denver from the late 1800s to the 1940s. For many years they played at Merchants Park, located near Broadway and Exposition, built in the 1920s. In 1947, the city offered land for a new ball-park at roughly 17th and Federal, which became Bears Stadium. Until 1993, the Bears (Zephyrs) shared that site with the Broncos. It became Mile High Stadium.

2. Bears become Zephyrs.
Efforts to bring a Major League franchise to Denver were thwarted time and again. There was talk that local oil tycoon Marvin Davis would buy the Oakland Athletics and relocate them. But the deal fell through. Real estate mogul John Dikeou and his brothers bought the Bears in 1984. They decided to call the team the Zephyrs. Fans said, "Huh?"

1. Rise of the Rockies.
It took a dedicated crowd of investors, politicians and fans—plus a stadium tax—to win a Major League franchise for the Mile High City in June 1991. But the owners didn't call the team the Denver Rockies as some had hoped. They were the Colorado Rockies.

Five Best Coaching Performances in Nuggets History :: Andrew Feinstein

Note: Andrew Feinstein, proprietor of FireGeorgeKarl.com, is a fourth-generation Denverite and self-professed Nuggets encyclopedia. He's also a co-creator of *Girls & Sports,* a nationally syndicated comic strip about dating and sports.

5. Dan Issel (1993-94.)

An all-time Nuggets legend as a player, Issel coached the NBA's youngest squad to 42 wins and they squeaked into the 8th seed in the NBA Playoffs. What followed was the biggest upset in NBA Playoff history at that time, when the Nuggets upset the 63-win Seattle Supersonics (coached by current Nuggets head coach George Karl) 3 games to 2, after getting crushed in the first two games. The Nuggets remarkable run would end in the second round but not without more drama, as they tied the Utah Jazz at three games apiece after being down 3 games to none.

4. Doug Moe (1987-88.)

Inarguably the greatest season in NBA history (as the league would expand to four more teams over the next two seasons, diluting the talent pool), Moe coached the Nuggets to their best NBA record with 54 wins and a Midwest Division title. Most unfortunately, a terrific regular season resulted in a disappointing postseason, as the Nuggets lost to the Dallas Mavericks in the playoffs' second round.

3. Doug Moe (1984-85.)

Moe coached the Nuggets to 52 wins and the franchise's only Western Conference Finals appearance, where the Nuggets lost to the Lakers 4 games to 1. The experience was so scarring for Moe and the Nuggets, that when they faced the Lakers in the playoffs' first round several seasons later, Moe would remark: "We got no shot to beat the Lakers."

2. Larry Brown (1975-76.)

In the final season of the American Basketball Association, Brown coached the Nuggets to a franchise second-best 60 wins and their only appearance in an ABA or NBA Finals, which they unfortunately lost to Julius Erving's New York Nets. When the Nuggets made their NBA debut the following season, their 50-win record was tied for the league's second-best regular season mark, but they lost in the semifinals to the eventual NBA Champion Portland Trailblazers.

1. Jeff Bzdelik (2002-03.)

Even though General Manager Kiki Vandeweghe purposely fielded the least talented team in NBA history in hopes of landing the #1 pick in the draft at season's end, Bzdelik remarkably coached the Nuggets to 17 wins—that's 17 more wins than they should have won. Bzdelik's roster was so bad that not only did the Nuggets hold open tryouts before the season began, but neither guard who made up the team's starting backcourt would appear in an NBA uniform the following season.

Note: Here's another list from the proprietor of FireGeorgeKarl.com. Notice who's not on the list.

5. Dan Issel / Mike Evans (2001-02.)

Even though Issel only coached 26 Nuggets games this season (before being forced to resign for calling a belligerent fan a "Mexican piece of s—-," the awful 27-win result is almost more his responsibility than Evans'. After all, Issel was also the General Manager who "built" the team with limited personnel resources due to terrible drafting and some inexcusably awful trades.

4. Bernie Bickerstaff / Dick Motta (1996-97.)

Poor Dick Motta. A former Bickerstaff mentor, Motta signed on for what he thought would be a cushy assistant coaching job at Bickerstaff's side. Instead, Bickerstaff quit on the Nuggets as coach one month into the season, and several months after taking a wrecking ball to whatever was left of the Nuggets once talented up-and-coming young roster. Motta was left to deal with the carnage, and "led" the Nuggets to a pathetic 21-win season, the franchise's fourth-worst ever.

3. Bernie Bickerstaff (1995-96.)

After putting together some suspect rosters during his tenure as Nuggets General Manager, Bickerstaff finally got the opportunity to prove that he was totally inept as a coach, too. Even though his young, talented roster featuring players like Dikembe Mutombo and Antonio McDyess made the playoffs the two previous seasons, Bickerstaff was able to under-coach them into a 35-win season. The following season, Bickerstaff would quit on the team as coach and then as GM, leaving the entire organization in shambles for Dick Motta.

2. Paul Westhead (1990-91.)

Westhead didn't just help prove the theory that college coaches universally fail in the NBA, he cemented it. In fairness to Westhead, his roster (put together by General Manager Bernie Bickerstaff—the Nuggets worst GM of all time) didn't give him a lot to work with. But Westhead employed a ludicrous up-tempo system that only benefited Nuggets opponents—like the Phoenix Suns who once scored 100 points against the Nuggets at halftime! Westhead's Nuggets put up an astounding 119.9 points a game. Of course, their opponents put up 130.8 ppg.

1. Bill Hanzlik (1997-98.)

Like Jeff Bzdelik, Hanzlik was sandbagged by his General Manager (in this case, Allan Bristow) with the least talented roster in the league. Unlike Bzdelik, Hanzlik did the least with an already bad situation, as he coached the Nuggets to a paltry 11 wins, tying the second-worst mark in NBA history. Before taking the head coaching job, several Denver newspaper columnists wrote that he should pass on this coaching "opportunity" . . . Hanz should've listened!

Note: John Hickenlooper was a successful entrepreneur before he became a politician. He developed Wynkoop Brewing Company, the first brewpub in the Rocky Mountains. He helped to revive LoDo, Denver's Lower Downtown historic district. In 2000, Hickenlooper led a grassroots campaign to preserve the Mile High Stadium name. The experience inspired him to run for mayor in 2003. Now in his second term, Hickenlooper is one of Denver's all-time most popular and accomplished mayors. Hizzoner is a life-long baseball fan. We asked him to list his most memorable baseball moments.

7. Steve Bartman catching the ball over Moises Alou, 2003.

An overzealous fan reached out and grabbed the ball. Who knows if Moises would have caught that ball or not, but the Cubs immediately fell apart following that moment. They never recovered in that game or the following game and went on to lose the series. The Cubs were leading the game 3-0 and the series 3 games to 2. They were 5 outs from beating the Marlins and going to the World Series for the first time since 1945 (and we Rockies fans thought we were going through a drought.) Many fans reached for the ball, but Bartman is credited for being the one who prevented Alou from having a shot at the ball. The Marlins went on to score 8 runs, 6 of them unearned. Marlins went on to win the series against Chicago and beat the Yankees to win the World Series.

6. George Brett charging the umpires in 1983 after Billy Martin accuses him of using too much pine tar on his bat.

Brett, an extremely competitive player and one of the greatest hitters of his time, did not take kindly to being called a cheater by the skipper of the Yankees. Brett's bat was examined by the umpires, and when they sided with Martin, Brett came charging out of the Royals dugout, veins protruding from his head and neck, red in the face and screaming. He was literally on fire.

5. Kirk Gibson, Dodgers, 1988.

The MVP spent the entire game in the clubhouse injured, yet came out in the 9th to hit a game-winning homerun against Dennis Eckersley. Tommy Lasorda held Gibson out of the game and did not even put him in the batter's box to warm up. No one expected him to play. I think this is probably the most memorable homerun in baseball history.

4. Bill Buckner, Red Sox, 1986 vs. the Mets.

Late in game 6 with Boston up, a routine ground ball hops through Buckner's legs. The Sox choked away that game and went on to lose the Series to the Miracle Mets. Only recently have those passionate Red Sox fans let up on poor Buckner.

3. Pete Rose charging the plate in all star game, 1970, separating and fracturing catcher Ray Fosse's shoulder.

To see All-Stars and legends of the game going all-out in the All-Star game shows how competitive these guys really were. I think we've lost some of that truly electric, competitive edge in today's game. Pete Rose rounded third base and charged for home plate, plowing into Ray Fosse like they were playing in the World Series.

2. Rockies Play-in Game, Oct. 1, 2007 vs. the San Diego Padres.

I was in San Antonio, Texas at the time and had to frantically rush out of an event to get to the hotel bar just in time to watch the last couple innings of the game. Up until that time, I had been receiving frequent updates via text messages and emails. This was truly one of the most riveting finishes to a season I have ever seen. For the Rockies to go down by three runs, then see Trevor Hoffman come in hoping to slam the door on the Rockies season truly seemed miraculous. 2007 was a magical season for those young men.

1. 1964 Phillies Pennant Chase: The worst late-season collapse in baseball history.

Lost 7 out of the last 10 and fell out of first in the home finale. I was a young boy grow-ing up in Philly at the time. I remember lying in bed, clutching my handheld radio and intently listening to the games. I listened to the final game on that radio, while huddled under my covers. . . . I almost rushed out of my room to jump off the roof following that loss.

Note: Denver native Dave Kopel is a columnist for the *Rocky Mountain News*, and research director for the *Independence Institute*.

10. 1962 losing season.

In the third season of the upstart American Football League, the Broncos charge out of the gate with a 6-1 record. After splitting the next pair of games, the Broncos lose all of their last five games to finish 7-7. In the first three AFL seasons, the Broncos have not had a single winning season. After 1962 there would be a decade of very rapid social changes in America, and in professional football. But there would still be a few constants: On Sunday evenings, families all over America would tune their televisions to *The Wonderful World of Disney*. On Sunday afternoons, an ever-growing number of fans would watch the Broncos establish themselves as one of the few teams in professional sports never to have had a winning season.

9. August 5, 1967, "little Super Bowl."

The previous January, Green Bay and Kansas City had played the first NFL vs. AFL game, in the Super Bowl. The new season's exhibition game between the Detroit Lions and the Broncos, at University of Denver Stadium, would be the first of what players would call the "little Super Bowls"—as the AFL tried to prove it was as good as the NFL, and the NFL strove to prove the opposite. Before the game, Detroit's star defensive tackle Alex Karras declared that if the Broncos won, he would walk home to Detroit. The Broncos did, 13-7, but Karras didn't.

8. August 18, 1967, beating the Vikings.

The Broncos beat another NFL team, the Minnesota Vikings, 13-9. Overall, the AFL finished 3-13 against the NFL in exhibition games in 1967, with the Broncos collecting 2/3 of the AFL's wins. Regular season AFL-NFL matchups would not take place until 1970, when the AFL was fully merged into the NFL.

7. September 10, 1967, start of another losing streak.

Although the Broncos have finished 4-10 in their previous two seasons, and 2-11-1 in the two seasons before that, hopes are high; new coach Lou Saban has led the team to a pair of exhibition wins against the mighty NFL. The Broncos start off the regular season by defeating the Boston Patriots. But the next week, the Broncos hit one of their lowest points ever as a competitive team, demolished 51-0 by the Oakland Raiders. The loss begins a 9-game losing streak, as Broncos revert to their usual standard of futility.

6. October 6, 1968, Briscoe leads the team.
The Broncos lose their first three games and three quarterbacks in 1968. Florida State University star Steve Tensi had been obtained from San Diego at the price of two first-round draft picks. But Tensi missed the first eight games due to an exhibition season injury, and the injury-plagued Tensi would never fulfill Denver's hopes. Both of the team's two backup quarterbacks were out with injuries by the fourth quarter of game three. Stepping into the fourth quarter of that game in Boston, 14th round draft pick Marlin "the Magician" Briscoe leads the team on a late drive, rushing 12 yards for the touchdown himself. In game four of the season, Briscoe takes the field in Denver as the first black starting quarterback in the AFL, and pilots the team to its first win of the season, over expansion team Cincinnati, who had embarrassed the Broncos by beating them three weeks before. Under Briscoe, the Broncos won four of five games, until Tensi returned, and the Broncos lost five of six. In Briscoe's single season with the Broncos, Briscoe would establish himself as the all-time best running quarterback in Broncos history—until Elway arrived in 1983.

5. Sept. 21, 1969, Broncos beat the best.
The world champion New York Jets, led by quarterback Broadway Joe Namath come to town for the second game of the season. The Broncos win 21-19.

4. Nov. 2, 1969, beating the Chargers.
The Broncos can beat the world champions. But can they beat anyone in their Division? For years the Broncos have been mired in fourth place in the AFL West. Although the Broncos win about half their games against other teams, they are regularly beaten season after season by Oakland, Kansas City, and San Diego—who, along with the Broncos, are the original teams of the AFL West. So it is a breakthrough in early November when the Broncos beat the San Diego Chargers 13-0, whom the Broncos had last defeated in 1966.

3. October 4, 1970, beating the Chiefs.
Eleven months after beating San Diego, the Broncos are the winners of a home game against the Kansas City Chiefs. It is the first time they have overcome the Chiefs since 1964.

2. October 22, 1972, beating the Raiders.
The Broncos win a 30-23 away game against the Oakland Raiders, their first victory over that team since the long-ago win streak in 1962. The triumph over their most dominant Western Division rival would eventually provide the margin for the Broncos to scrape their way into third place in the Western Division—a change from nine consecutive seasons of fourth-place finishes.

1. 1973, breaking the loser curse.
Second-year coach John Ralston leads the Broncos to the 7-5-2 record, with the team remaining in contention for the AFC West until the last game of the season. UPI names Ralston AFC Coach of the Year. The Broncos are far from being champions, but they have at last escaped their status as perennial losers.

Superstar racecar driver and sports commentator Bobby Unser was born in Colorado Springs, Colorado. He's a member of the International Motorsports Hall of Fame and the Indy 500 Hall of Fame. You probably didn't know that he also served in the U.S. Air Force. Here's a list of some of Bobby's accomplishments behind the wheel.

10. In 1968, he was the first driver to run faster than 170 mph at Indianapolis.

9. Average speed in 1972: 201.374 mph.

That year, Bobby was the first driver ever to record a qualifying average speed over 200 mph in Indy car competition.

8. New record in 1993: 223.709 mph.

That's the land speed record Bobby set at Bonneville Salt Flats in 1993 with a gas-powered modified roadster.

7. Two-time series winner of the International Race of Champions.

6. California 500 wins: 4.

In 1974, 1976, 1979 and 1980.

5. Two-time National Champion.

In 1968 and 1974.

4. Career Pole Positions: 49.

3. Pikes Peak Hill Climb winner 13 times.

That's a record number of titles. Bobby is the only driver in the history of the race to win all three divisions: open wheel racing, stock cars and sports cars.

2. Career Indy Car Victories: 35.

1. Indy 500 Champion: 3 times.

In 1968, 1975 and 1981.

Note: Bobby Unser won a record 13 titles at the Pikes Peak International Hill Climb in Colorado Springs. He's the undisputed King of the Mountain. The race started in 1916, making it the second oldest race in U.S. history. (The Indy 500 is the oldest.) Cars sprint 12.4 miles up Pikes Peak to a finish line 14,110 feet above sea level. The twisting road and high altitude make it one of the toughest races in the world. We asked Bobby to list a few things you might not know about him and the Race to the Clouds.

4. My family has a long history on the mountain.

In 1915, my dad and his brothers, Louis and Joe, rode motorcycles to the top of Pikes Peak. My Uncle Louis was my hero. He raced Pikes Peak every year. He won the race nine times between the time I was born and the day I turned thirteen. My childhood dream was to drive that race. When I was 16, I remember watching Uncle Louis race, and I remember thinking that I could do better than him. I started thinking about how I would win the race one day. I even told him, "I'm going to be the new king of this mountain." I started racing there in 1955. Some people call Pikes Peak "Unser Mountain" because so many Unser brothers, sons, grandsons and nephews have raced there.

3. Pressure brings out the best in me.

In 1959, I had about $1,000 to my name and a family to support. I spent $1,000 on a chance to buy and build my own car for the Hill Climb. I *had* to win the race and the $10,000 purse—that was my only option. I set a new course record that year, winning the Open Class race in 13 minutes and 36 seconds.

2. Pikes Peak taught me to expect the unexpected.

Because of the change in elevation from start to finish, you can be driving in hot, dusty summer weather, then springtime rain and mud, then winter snow—all within the same race. I suffer from allergies, so I never knew when the dust and pollen on the mountain would irritate my eyes and swell my sinuses. Sometimes, fans would get too close to the road. One time, a fan was in the middle of the track, trying to get a good picture, or something. I had to swerve. My car could have gone over the side. You never know what's going to be on the track—rocks, patches of gravel, places torn up by previous drivers going up the hill. It's the most challenging and the most fun race I've ever run.

1. Bill Daniels sponsored my final Hill Climb in 1986.

The previous year, my Hill Climb record had been broken by a young French woman, the most successful and well-known female rally driver of the time and the only woman to win a round of the World Rally Championship. I was 52 years old, but I was not going to let her record stand. Audi offered me a car, but I needed sponsorship. Denver cable TV magnate and all-around good guy Bill Daniels came through for me at the last minute. Audi is a German car, but Bill made sure it was decked out in American red, white and blue. My allergies brought me misery on race day, but I won. I also set a new record. I didn't want to be beat by a woman driver from France.

Note: Michael Booth has written about movies for *The Denver Post* for the past six years, and is the author of *The Denver Post Guide to the Best Family Films: 52 Great Movies to Fill Up Your Year.*

15. *Remember the Titans.*

Under the withering gaze of Denzel Washington, a racially mixed group of high school athletes struggles with desegregation. An appealing mix of politics, morality and gamesmanship.

14. *Pride of the Yankees.*

If only to memorialize an era when an athlete could be an untarnished hero, the story of the Iron Horse stands the test of time. Gary Cooper made Lou Gehrig's iconic status a permanent phenomenon.

13. *Tin Cup.*

Kevin Costner again—see #8 and #7—is there a theme here? Yes—Kevin, stick to the sports movies. From the same writer as *Bull Durham*, this laidback romantic comedy invents some personality for the bland PGA tour.

12. *Hoop Dreams.*

This acclaimed documentary reveals the cynicism that, no matter how infuriating, can't quite undermine the excitement of bigtime sports programs.

11. *Kingpin.*

Safe to say it's the only great bowling movie. There may not be much sport here, but it's one of the most hilarious crude comedies ever made. Bill Murray's unwinding combover is worth the entire price.

10. *The Heart of the Game.*

This little-known basketball documentary is the kind of fact no one would buy as fiction. A Seattle girls' basketball team follows its quirky coach through a drama of mistakes and redemption.

9. *Miracle.*

The other great hockey movie. It took decades to recapture the 1980 Olympic stunner in a feature movie, but the wait was worth it, with Kurt Russell nearly matching the intensity of late legend Herb Brooks.

8. *Bull Durham.*

Susan Sarandon made sports movies sexy for once. She made every wannabe jock long for a hometown athletic supporter. A stellar cast, with Kevin Costner and Tim Robbins, put soul in a terrific comedy.

7. *Field of Dreams.*

Go ahead, see if you can watch all the way to the end without crying. As stuffed with corn as that field Kevin Costner plows under to build a diamond, the movie nevertheless captures the pain and longing of adulthood.

6. *Caddyshack.*
Maybe it's not a sports movie. But then, maybe golf isn't actually a sport. Rodney Dangerfield and Bill Murray compete to see who can steal the most scenes in this beloved romp.

5. *North Dallas Forty.*
One of the few great football movies, this gritty, wide-open view of life on the gridiron fore-told the cynicism of the steroids era. A signature role for Nick Nolte.

4. *Breaking Away.*
Long before Greg LeMond and Lance Armstrong convinced disdainful American fans that cycling requires a lion's heart, this goofy take on adolescence, youth and ambition won over the moviegoing public.

3. *The Natural.*
Baseball movies as a group are the best sports films, perhaps because they're the eas-iest to fake. But there's nothing artificial about this melancholy, archetypal adaptation of Bernard Malamud's novel. Some say that Robert Redford perfected his swing on a base-ball scholarship at the University of Colorado.

2. *Slap Shot.*
Not just the only great hockey movie—also one of the great all-time comedies. Paul Newman took a B-movie script to the A level, and beyond.

1. *Hoosiers.*
If the best sports legends began as real-life fairy tales, then this smalltown-heroes story must top the list. Its sweat-stained look at Indiana basketball mania reminds Americans how they want to think of themselves.

Our Top Ten Sports Movies

Folks love to debate this category. Everyone has a favorite line or favorite scene that strikes a chord and lifts one movie above another. It's highly subjective . . . whereas our opinions about everything else are purely rational and scientific.

10. *Rocky.*
The first one, from 1976. The fight scenes were terrific. The scene where Stallone is punching out the meat in the cooler—how can anyone forget the ferocity of that? Paulie says, "You do that to Apollo Creed, they'll put us in jail for murder." Also, Mickey tells Rocky, "You're gonna eat lightning and you're gonna crap thunder."

9. *The Longest Yard.*
The 1974 original with Burt Reynolds. "We're gettin' up a football game against the guards. Wondered if maybe you and some of your buddies here would like to join in on the fun." Eddie Albert was perfect as the sleazy warden.

8. *Rudy.*
Sean Astin captured the dream of every undersized kid in America. "I'm here to play football for the Irish."

7. *Cinderella Man.*
Russell Crowe was simply brilliant. "You think you're telling me something? Boxing is dangerous, something like that? You don't think working triple shifts and at night on a scaffold isn't just as likely to get a man killed?" Another great scene: "I believe we live in a great country, a country that's great enough to help a man financially when he's in trouble. But lately, I've had some good fortune, and I'm back in the black. I just thought I should return it."

6. *The Hustler.*
1961. The three heavyweight stars were great. Loved several lines. Jackie Gleason: "Fast Eddie, let's play some pool." George C. Scott: "Stay with this kid. He's a loser." Newman was as good in this one as he was in *Slap Shot.*

5. *The Bad News Bears.*
1976. As funny as Bears is, it's not far from the truth of what the world of Little League baseball is all about—the coaches, the kids, the parents. It's a small comedy, but we would rank Walter Matthau's performance as grumpy, drinking Coach Buttermaker with any performance of his career, which is saying a lot. Tatum O'Neal, Vic Morrow, Jackie Earle Haley, and Chris Barnes as Tanner lead a strong ensemble cast. A kid asks, "If you were so great, how come you never made it to the major leagues?" Buttermaker replies, "Contract disputes."

4. *The Natural.*
Loved Redford's line, "I want to walk down the street and the people say 'There goes Roy Hobbs, the best there ever was.'" Loved Wilfred Brimley as the manager and his line, "I should have been a farmer." By the way, it's often said that Robert Redford played baseball at the University of Colorado. But according to Frank "The Chief" Prentup, it didn't happen. Irv took Prentup's position coaching at CU, so he would know. Sorry to debunk

this bit of movie/baseball folklore.

3. *Slap Shot.*
1977. Just to hear Maxine Nightingale sing Right Back Where We Started From over and over was worth it. The Hanson brothers made us laugh and Paul Newman was believable. Hyannisport broadcaster: "Look at that. You can't see that, I'm on radio."

2. *Raging Bull.*
DeNiro's portrayal of Jake LaMotta was incredible. He put on a ton of weight to show how LaMotta went to the bottom. Joe Pesci was solid as the brother. Remember when Jake takes a beating but stays on his feet and says, "You didn't get me down, Ray." Powerful.

1. *Hoosiers.*
Great nostalgia. The way Gene Hackman captured coach Norman Dale was a classic. The movie is based on the 1954 Indiana State High School champs, the Milan Indians. It's for all the little schools who never got a chance to play for the big one. The old gyms, the short shorts, the referees' long sleeve shirts, the hangers-on . . . It was truly a classic. "My practices aren't designed for your enjoyment."

Most Memorable Athlete Performances in Movies
:: Michael Booth

Note: A bonus list from *The Denver Post* scribe. "Memorable" is a great word. It's like "interesting." It can mean anything.

15. O.J. Simpson in *Capricorn One.*
14. Duane The Rock Johnson in *The Mummy* and *Rundown.*
13. Shaquille O'Neal in *Kazaam.*
12. Cam Neeley in *Dumb and Dumber.*
11. Dan Marino in *Ace Ventura, Pet Detective.*
10. Mike Ricci in *The Rocket.*
9. Michael Jordan in *Space Jam.*
8. Bob Uecker in the *Major League* movies.
7. Alex Karras in *Blazing Saddles.*
6. Randall "Tex" Cobb in *Raising Arizona.*
5. Brett Favre in *There's Something About Mary.*
4. Johnny Weissmuller in the Tarzan movies.
3. Arnold Schwarzenegger in *The Terminator* films.
2. Andre the Giant in *Princess Bride.*
1. Kareem Abdul-Jabbar in *Airplane!*

When I was a coach and went to coaching clinics, the strategy and X-and-O chalk talks were okay. But I came to life when the speaker talked about the intangibles—attitude, perseverance, practice time, and how to treat your players. That's what these movies convey. I have seen these movies many times, and I could watch them again.

4. *Cinderella Man.*

The thing that impresses me: Throughout everything that goes on in this movie, James J. Braddock stays so humble. It's the quality you love in an athlete, and it's pretty rare. He fought for all the right reasons—for food and clothing and housing for his family. He didn't fight for notoriety, which never lasts anyway.

3. *Million Dollar Baby.*

At first Clint Eastwood wants nothing to do with coaching a woman. But he watches her. He sees a work ethic and he sees talent, and that's what excites every coach. We all think we can make someone into a special athlete when we see that. *Million Dollar Baby* got across the perfect feel for the special relationship that can develop between a coach and an athlete.

2. *Glory Road.*

The story of Texas Western, an all-black team that beat an all-white team in the NCAA Finals. The story and movie meant a lot to me personally because I was the referee in many of those games. Two of my boys played football at the school. Don Haskins is in the Basketball Hall of Fame and he broke through a lot of barriers. The movie was pretty factual. Hollywood captured the trainer, Ross Moore, as well as anyone could.

1. *Hoosiers.*

To me, this is the perfect example of a coach accommodating his players and the players learning to perform for him. My favorite scene is in the title game, when Coach Norman Dale calls the final play—a shot for one of his supporting players. His team keeps staring at him, doesn't move, until the coach says, "What?" The players all look to another teammate, Jimmy Chitwood, their star, who simply says to the coach, "I'll make it." So Coach Dale, listening to his team, changes the play. And of course, Jimmy hits the winning shot. Sometimes a coach has to listen to his team.

Joe's Five Favorite College Football Films

These are my personal favorites out of a long list of great sports flicks.

5. *Everybody's All-American.*
1988. Screen adaptation of Frank DeFord's novel, The Rise and Fall of a Southern Football Hero. Denver has a cameo when Dennis Quaid appears in a Broncos uniform.

4. *The Program.*
1993. Starring James Caan. Many former college players regard this one as the most accurate portrayal of Division One Football. A memorable exchange: "This is not a football vocational school. It's an institute for higher learning." "Yeah, but when was the last time 80,000 people showed up to watch a kid do a damn chemistry experiment?"

3. *Horse Feathers.*
1932. Starring Groucho Marx. Huxley College fields a team to beat a rival school . . . with hilarious consequences. Dialogue: "Oh, Professor, you're full of whimsy." "Can you notice it from there? I'm always that way after I eat radishes."

2. *Knute Rockne, All-American.*
1940. "Win one for the Gipper." Starring Ronald Reagan as George Gipp and Pat O'Brien as Knute Rockne. Though highly inaccurate, it was the most important sports film of its day. A product of the Notre Dame propaganda machine. Memorable line: "We haven't got any use for gamblers around here. You've done your best to ruin baseball, and horse racing, and this is one game that's clean and is gonna stay clean."

1. *Rudy.*
1993. A feel-good film for all Notre Dame haters. An adaptation of the life of Daniel "Rudy" Ruettiger. Had it not been true, no one would have ever believe it. Coach Parseghian: "If you had a tenth of the heart of Ruettiger, you'd have made All-American by now. As it is, you just went from third team to the scout team. Get out of here."

Best Sports Movies According to Our Listeners

We polled our audience for their favorite sports movies of all time. Here are movies they mentioned that aren't included on another list. In no particular order:

Brian's Song (1970) with James Caan, Billy Dee Williams.
A League of Their Own (1992) with Tom Hanks, Geena Davis.
Chariots of Fire (1981) with Ben Cross, Ian Charleston.
Eight Men Out (1988) with Charlie Sheen, John Cusack.
Heaven Can Wait (1979) with Warren Beatty, Julie Christie.
Requiem for a Heavyweight (1962) with Anthony Quinn, Jackie Gleason.
Bang the Drum Slowly (1973) with Robert DeNiro, Michael Moriarty.
Jerry Maguire (1997) with Tom Cruise, Cuba Gooding, Jr.
When We Were Kings (1996), Documentary.
Karate Kid (1984) with Ralph Macchio, Pat Morita.
61* (2001) with Barry Pepper, Thomas Jane.
One Day in September (2002), Documentary.
Paper Lion (1968) with Alan Alda, Lauren Hutton.
White Men Can't Jump (1992) with Wesley Snipes, Woody Harrelson.
One on One (1980) with Robby Benson, Annette O'Toole.
The Color of Money (1986) with Paul Newman, Jackie Gleason.
All the Right Moves (1983) with Tom Cruise, Lea Thompson.
National Velvet (1944) with Elizabeth Taylor, Mickey Rooney.
Vision Quest (1985) with Matthew Modine, Linda Fiorentino.
The Hurricane (1999) with Denzel Washington, Dan Hedaya.
Semi-Tough (1977) with Burt Reynolds, Kris Kristofferson.
Damn Yankees (1958) with Gwen Verdon, Tab Hunter.
Fever Pitch (1997) with Colin Firth, Ken Stott.
Gentleman Jim (1942) with Errol Flynn, Alexis Smith.
Major League (1989) with Tom Berenger, Charlie Sheen.
The Rookie (2002) with Dennis Quaid, Rachel Griffiths.
Victory (1981) with Sylvester Stallone, Michael Caine.
Body and Soul (1947) with John Garfield, Lilli Palmer.
Without Limits (1998) with Billy Crudup, Donald Sutherland.
Downhill Racer (1969) with Robert Redford, Gene Hackman.

Note: Dorothy Mauk was a long time sports writer for *The Denver Post*. She was inducted into the Colorado Tennis Hall of Fame in 2002. As a member of the Colorado Sports Hall of Fame Selection Committee, she has championed women athletes. Here are her all-time top picks.

13. Jill McGill (Cherry Creek High School/USC)—Golf.

With golf becoming a sanctioned sport for girls in her senior year (1990), she led the Bruins to the state title. Moving on to USC, she was named a Second Team All-America in her sophomore year, but the summer of 1993 was her season to remember. She reached the semifinals of the U.S. Women's Amateur Public Links Championship at Jackson Hole and the Broadmoor Invitational, and won the 93rd U.S. Women's Amateur Championship for the most coveted crown in women's amateur golf. The latter gave her an automatic berth in the 1994 U.S. Women's Open Championship. She also was named to the U.S. team for Curtis Cup play matching the eight best U.S. amateur players again their counterparts from Britain and Ireland. She was awarded her LPGA card in 1998.

12. Debbie Wilcox (Littleton)—Gymnastics.

Although she had taken up gymnastics just four years earlier (1972), she already was a Top 10 finisher in the Elite Class of U.S. Gymnastics Federation (USGF) competition and a member of the fourth-place U.S. team in the 1975 Pan-Am Games when she went to Montreal for the 1976 Summer Games and finished 10 places higher than any previous U.S. gymnast in Olympic competition. Although the meet marked the demise of Olga Korbut and ascendance of Nadia Comaneci and will be remembered as the first to record a perfect 10.0 Olympic score, it also was the first to showcase a consistently competitive U.S. performance with Wilcox's 9.6 on vault, 9.5 on floor ex, 9.45 on uneven parallel bars and 9.25 on balance beam for an 18th place, 37.80-point-all-around total. Wilcox got to Montreal by placing fourth in individual Olympic qualifying and winning a U.S. vs. Canada dual-meet-all-around title in Olympic team qualifying. In addition to her Olympic accomplishments, the 17-year-old won the 1976 South Africa Cup championship, finished third behind Nadia and another Romanian in the all-around standing of a qualifying meet at Tucson, repeated as USGF National uneven bars champion and maintained her Top 10 status in Elite Masters national competition.

11. Kirsten Hanssen (Denver)—Triathlon.

When the 1988 triathlon season began, this five-foot-three Wonder Woman owned 16 titles, including the World championship, and dominated all distances international, long and sprint. She was the first woman ever to win back-to-back U.S. National titles, the first to win two Triple Crown races in one year, and the only U.S. athlete to win the Nationals and Grand Prix Cumulative Points Series two years in a row. In 1987 alone, she had earned more than $100,000 in prizes and endorsements. Continuing her torrid pace in 1988, the 1987 Triathlete of the Year upset the defending champion in the Mountain Man Winter Triathlon and won the $105,000 America's Paradise spectacular. She seemed invincible . . . until tendonitis struck both of her knees. She was back in the winner's circle by June, but an automobile accident in July left her with two broken wrist bones, a skinned side and an arm cast to wear for the rest of the year. With her hopes for National and Grand Prix three-peats sidelined, the 26-year-old Coloradan called upon her towering inner strength to overcome the injuries and regain her No. 1 status. Winning five more short-course races, she managed to finish a close second in both the year-end points standings and Triathlete of the Year polls. The highlight of her tireless endeavor was her debut in the Ironman (Long-Course) Triathlon in Hawaii. Although handicapped by her cast in the first two events, she still finished third in the women's final standings (two minutes off the course record), trailed only the 1986 and 1987 winners and was the No. 1 American woman (63rd finisher among all participants).

10. Amy Van Dyken (Cherry Creek High School)—Swimming.

The fastest female swimmer in the history of the U.S. first gained recognition at Cherry Creek High School as a six-time-all-America, Athlete of the Year and winner of State, Junior National and Olympic Festival championships even though she couldn't swim across the pool until she was 12 because of asthma challenges. The greatest influence on her career development, however, wasn't overcoming her health concerns but her 1993 transfer from the University of Arizona to CSU in 1993. By 1994, she was a 19-time all-America, WAC Female Athlete of the Year, NCAA champion, American record-holder in the 50-yard freestyle and NCAA-II Swimmer of the Year. In her first venture overseas, she captured three World Championship medals and set an American record at Rome. She then won her sprint specialty at the U.S. Open and made the U.S. National Team. The lean six-footer gave an even more spectacular performance in 1995, bettering the American short-course mark for the 50-yard freestyle, twice eclipsing the American and U.S. Open records for the 50-meter freestyle and successfully defending her U.S. National freestyle title. After she also established a World short-course standard for the 50 butterfly in Finland, won three golds and silver in the Pan-Am Games and brought home two golds and silver from the Pan-Pacific Championships, she was #1 in the World and Swimming magazine's 1995 Swimmer of the Year. She then won four gold medals in the 1996 Summer Games at Atlanta, more than any woman ever had collected in a single Olympics, but didn't retire until after the 1998 World meet. In 2001, she entered the Colorado Sports Hall of Fame (CSHOF.)

9. Ellen Miller (Vail)—Mountain Sports.

An athlete like no other, this Vail Athletic Club instructor and coach competes in and teaches everything from running and mountain biking to snowshoeing and Nordic skiing. But she also is into things that have never been done before, like eclipsing the World record (in 1998) for Highest Altitude Ski Descent on Mustagh-Ata mountain in China and becoming the first U.S. woman to scale Mt. Everest from the north side (in 2002) and then doing it from the south side a few months later to become the first North American woman ever to reach the summit of Mt. Everest twice, in the same year! Moving to Colorado in 1980 at age 21, she started climbing the state's fourteeners almost non-stop. Summiting all 54 in five years, she moved on to Mt. Ranier, Mt. Shasta, Denali, Mont Blanc (France), Kilimanjaro (Tanzania), Cotopaxi and Chimborazo (both Ecuador), Mt. Elbrus (Russia), Aconcagua (Argentina) and Cho-Oyu (Nepal-Tibet). To this athlete who favors the impossible, a foot race is more apt to mean the Leadville 100-mile run than a 10K jog and a hike could be a three-month trek along the Continental Divide, not a park stroll! Endurance obviously is her middle name.

8. April Heinrichs (Littleton)—Soccer.

While at Littleton's Heritage High School, she was the best girl soccer player in Colorado. Leading the Eagles to four league titles (1979-82) and two state championships (1979, 1981), she was All-Conference three times, All-State twice and All-America once. At the

University of North Carolina, where she was a three-time First Team All-America, she did more than spark the Tar Heels to an 85-3-2 record, three NCAA titles and one runner-up finish. She became the NCAA's all-time leading scorer with 87 goals in 90 games and UNC's first female player to have her number retired. She made more soccer history in 1991 as captain and top scorer of the winning U.S. team in the first-ever Women's World Cup tournament in China. In 1998, she became the first woman player inducted into the National Soccer Hall of Fame. Mirroring her playing success is a coaching career reflecting a 10-year 116-73-15 collegiate record, membership on the coaching staff that led the USA to its first-ever gold medal in the 1996 Olympics and a four-year term as head coach of the U-16 National Team. In January 2000, she became head coach of the U.S. Women's National Team, the first female in the program's 17-year history. Her five-year 87-17-20 tenure ended with a second Olympic gold medal in 2004 and CSHOF induction in 2005.

7. Dorothy Hamill (Denver)—Figure Skating.

The former Colorado Academy student, who was reared in Connecticut but trained at Colorado Ice Arena in Denver through most of her amateur career, logged performances in 20 nations by age 20. She won 15 major titles between 1969 and 1975, including the International Grand Prix at St. Gervais, Nebelhorn Trophy (Oberstdorf), Richmond Trophy (London) and Prague Skate Invitational. Her competitive career reached its zenith in 1976 when she captured a third consecutive U.S. National Senior Ladies crown, the World championship at Gothenburg, Sweden, and a gold medal at the Winter Olympic Games in Innsbruck, Austria. After making the Hamill Camel spin and Hamill Haircut household words, the celebrated amateur princess achieved professional stardom with Ice Capades.

6. Tanya Haave (Evergreen)—Basketball/Volleyball.

The Evergreen High School/University of Tennessee star set the standard for Colorado athletes as a prepster and then established herself at the top of the collegiate and professional ranks, too. In her final season of prep basketball, she sparked the Cougars to third-place at State as well as a 60-10 total mark and set four state-tournament scoring records, including a perfect 100 single-game free throw percentage. She was Player of the Year a second straight time and, not surprisingly, made all of the national All-America lists. Her prep volleyball teams compiled a 67-9 tally, including a string of 52 consecutive wins in her final two seasons. As team leader at the net, Haave topped all classification levels of the state in kills and blocks throughout her Evergreen career. She got off to an equally fast collegiate start. In her freshman season of AIAW volleyball, she eclipsed the Tennessee school spiking record with 38 in one match, had the best serving efficiency rating on the varsity squad and led all the statistical categories. (She may still hold the UT records for kills and kill attempts.) With a full-ride scholarship for basketball, however, she zeroed in on it. A three-year starter, the 6-foot-2 forward propelled the Lady Vols to three Final Fours and two title games, graduating as UT's all-time career scoring leader and Player of the Game for 1984's NCAA title match. Punctuating her undergraduate years were berths on a gold medal National Sports Festival Team, Junior National Team and National Jones Cup Team. She also was a Pan-Am finalist and Olympic Trials selectee. After her 1985 UT graduation, she played pro basketball for 14 years in France, Italy, Spain, Sweden and Australia, collecting an array of international accolades. The 12-time pro all-star spent one year as a head coach in Sweden before returning home to become an assistant coach at Regis University and then a member of Ceal Barry's staff at the University of Colorado. She's a 2004 CSHOF inductee.

5. Jayne Gibson (raised in Arvada)—Volleyball.

Excelling in basketball, track and field and volleyball, this multi-lettered, multi-titled and multi-talented standout was a member of three Class AAA State High School Tournament teams in 1977, but volleyball was her preferred sport. Leading her Arvada West squad to the league title and Class AAA state high school championship with a 24-2 record, the Wildcat senior was named to the all-league and all-state teams, was chosen state tournament MVP and was Colorado Sidelines player of the year as well as the Steinmark Trophy winner. Her RMAAU team, the Colorado Suns, reached the National Junior Olympic finals and she was dubbed best hitter-blocker in the RMAAU qualifying tournament. Quickly becoming a collegiate star at the University of the Pacific, she garnered multiple all-conference, all-America and all-tournament honors and was a three-time USVBA all-America. Her international exploits include silver medals in the Pacific Rim and NORCECA Championships, a bronze medal in the 1987 Pan Am Games, four years on the U.S. National Team and membership on the 1988 7th place U.S. Women's Olympic Team. After one pro season with the San Jose Gold Diggers in 1989, she began her coaching career with the UOP women's volleyball team. (I don't know where she is now.)

4. Alison Dunlap (Colorado Springs, raised in Aurora)—Mountain Biking.

Disappointed not to make the Colorado College soccer team, the Smoky Hill High School star switched to road cycling and went on to capture the 1991 NCAA championship, make the 1992 Olympic Trials and qualify No. 3 for the 1996 Summer Games. Taking up mountain biking after Atlanta, she rode to Pan Am gold in 1999 and 7th place at the 2000 Sydney Olympics. In 2001, the 32-year-old two-time Olympian was a top-three finisher in four of six major races and added the World title to garner year-end rankings of No. 4 in the World and No. 6 in World Cup competition. Two wins also gave her a No. 5 ranking on the U.S. National Short Track Series. Continuing to be a force on the road circuit as well, she posted major wins in Oregon, California and Idaho to win the third stage of the International Women's Challenge for the third time in her career and then made U.S. women's cycling history with a 5th straight U.S. Cyclo-Cross championship earning a berth on the 2002 U.S. World Cyclo-Cross Team. At year-end, she was nominated by USA Cycling for the 72nd annual AAU Sullivan Award and 2001 U.S. Olympic Sportswoman of the Year Award.

3. Connie Carpenter-Phinney (Boulder)—Cycling (Road).

She got her first taste of Olympic competition as a U.S. speed skater in 1972 at Sapporo, but by 1977, this determined redhead owned nearly every major title in women's cycling including the U.S. Road Racing Championship, first of 11 National titles on her ledger. Moving to Colorado permanently in 1982, after a brief 1980 stint on the UC-Berkeley rowing team, she became the dominant woman in cycling with a third straight Coors Classic victory, third consecutive World silver medal, top honors in the seven-race Self Series and second silver medal in the U.S. National Time Trails, a feat earning the Southland Olympic Award as Best Female Cyclist in America. In 1984 at Los Angeles, she bridged a 12-year gap in Olympic appearances with a road racing victory capping the Summer Games debut of women's cycling and ending a 72-year drought for U.S. cycling teams. She's a 1995 CSHOF inductee.

2. Rhonda Blanford-Green (Aurora/Parker)—Track.

This Aurora Central prep standout and University of Nebraska team captain was undefeated in Big Eight indoor and outdoor hurdles. In 1985 she captured her fourth consecutive Big Eight indoor crown (6 barriers) with a world-best clocking of 7.44 seconds (3rd best time ever for 60 meters) and added NCAA-I honors with a 7.57. Outdoors the same year, she annexed five 100-meter invitational titles in five different states before donning Big 8 laurels for 10 barriers, setting a Nebraska school record enroute and leaving three Olympians in her dust. Her 12.85 triumph at The Athletics Congress (TAC) Nationals was not only the fastest by an American in 1985 but also 9th fastest in the world. The Coloradoan completed her itinerary with a winning National Sports Festival stop and command performances in Japan and Germany as No. 1 hurdler on the USA Team. Currently, she's a Colorado High School Activities Association assistant commissioner.

1. Carol Baily (Steamboat Springs)—Tennis.

Colorado Rocky Mountain School alum and two-time national championship team member at Arizona State dominated state amateur competition, winning a combined 41 singles and doubles titles in Colorado's three major tournaments. Beginning at age 35, she won an additional 28 national Age Group championships over 15 years and, throughout the 1990s, was ranked #1 in the nation in both singles and doubles for her age division. In 1991 and 1995, she also was ranked #1 in the world for her age group. All that competition took a toll on her knees, so she's currently teaching fulltime while getting rebuilt.

Top Five Early Rockies

In 1991, the National League of Professional Baseball Clubs approved Denver for an expansion team to start playing in 1993. The Rockies broke the all-time attendance mark in that first year, drawing 4,483,350 fans. The New York Yankees and Toronto Blue Jays are the only other teams to surpass four million in total attendance in one season. Since 1993, the Rockies have continued to pace the entire league when it comes to drawing fans. From 1993 to 2006, Colorado's home attendance exceeded 44 million—better than any other team in baseball during that span. At Coors Field, we were number one in attendance for seven straight years until 1999. There was a steady decline going into the World Series year in 2007.

We expect attendance to shoot back up to record levels in coming seasons. The popularity of players such as Todd Helton, Matt Holliday and Troy Tulowitski has skyrocketed. Newer fans might not remember some of the early Rockies, but they're worth remembering. General Manager Bob Gebhardt did a great job with the expansion draft in 1993–1994. It was the start of the Blake Street Bombers, the lineup that would lead the National League in homeruns from 1995-1997. Man, they were fun.

5. Eric Young.

He gave you a day's work every time he took the field. He's still the career stolen-bases leader with 180. In 1996, he was the NL stolen-base champ with 53. That year, he hit .324 with 8 homeruns and 74 RBIs. Who can forget opening day 1993 at Mile High Stadium? The Rockies hosted Montreal with a record-setting crowd of 80,227. Young homered off Kent Bottenfield to open the game.

4. Ellis Burks.

The quiet man. He was one of Don Baylor's favorites. His approach to the game was special to see. Can't forget his inside-the-park homerun against Jeff Fassero from Montreal. In 1996 he had 142 runs, 40 homers, 32 stolen bases, 93 extra bases and 128 RBIs. Came in third in the MVP vote. Rox traded him to the Giants in 1998.

3. Dante Bichette.

The guy was always adjusting his batting gloves. He hit a lot of homeruns in Denver—21 in that first season. The best one was the walk-off against the Mets in the 1995 opener, his first homerun at Coors Field. In 1996, he and Ellis Burks both hit at least 30 homeruns and stole at least 30 bases. It doesn't happen often that two guys on the same team pull that off. Rox sent him to Cincinnati in 1999. Bichette also had a good arm. He pitched for a while in an independent league. His restaurant on 17th wasn't bad. The place closed but the sign with his name on it stayed up long after he'd left town.

2. Vinny Castilla.

He was out of position the first year. He didn't have the range to play shortstop. It was perfect when he moved to third. He had an accurate arm and hit the ball out of the park. He hit 132 homeruns at Coors Field, number three all time behind Todd Helton and Larry Walker.

1. Andres Galarraga.

The Big Cat. He's the only Rockie in the Colorado Sports Hall of Fame. He once had six hits in a game. He's number five in homeruns at Coors Field with 73. Hit over 30 home-runs three times. Had 150 RBIs in 1996. El Gato Grande—or is it El Gran Gato . . . ? He was a tremendously popular Rockie from 1993 to 1997. Rox released him in 1998. He went to Atlanta.

Note: Author and journalist Terry Frei knows all manner of fascinating facts about hockey in Denver, such as . . . .

6. When the word broke in mid 1995 that Comsat, the corporate owner of the NBA Nuggets, was purchasing the National Hockey League's Quebec Nordiques and moving the franchise to Denver, it was our second chance in the NHL.

5. The Colorado Rockies, not the guys in pinstripes, but in hockey uniforms, played in Denver for six seasons, from 1976-77 through 1981-82.

It was a rocky road, all right, with the Rockies making the playoffs only once in a league that didn't exactly set the bar high for postseason participation.

4. Though the Rockies had a host of good players, including Barry Beck, Wilf Paiement and especially future Hall of Famer Lanny McDonald, they traded most of them, often for each other, in panic-stricken moves.

3. The most games they ever won in a regular season was 22.

Attendance frequently was low, but the most galling reaction to that, an attitude that something was wrong with Denver as a hockey market if it wouldn't pack the arena for a terrible team, was reflective of the NHL's attitudes and problems of the time.

2. The original owner was Jack Vickers.

He would go on to make a more significant sporting mark with his International golf tournament at Castle Pines. He bailed out after two seasons, and the team was passed on to New Jersey trucking company owner Arthur Imperatore and, then, Buffalo cable television magnate Peter Gilbert.

1. Finally, and perhaps mercifully, the NHL approved Gilbert's sale of the franchise to John McMullen, who paid a king's ransom in territorial indemnities and moved the franchise to the Meadowlands sports complex, where they became the Devils.

As it turned out, the joke to a point was on McMullen, since the Devils developed into an NHL power, but never drew in the Meadowlands as well as a team of that caliber would have in Denver. And that wasn't prejudiced hot air, because the Avalanche quickly became a hot ticket in Denver. Yes, we were delivered a young and talented team, an immediate Stanley Cup contender.

Three Things You Probably Didn't Know About the Broncos :: Jim Saccomano

Note: Jim Saccomano has been with the Denver Broncos for more than 30 years. He is the club's primary spokesman. Before joining the Broncos in 1978, he directed public relations for the Denver Bears baseball team. He also chairs the Colorado Sports Hall of Fame. We asked him to list three things you probably didn't know about the Broncos. Broncos fans know absolutely everything, so Jim had his work cut out for him.

3. The original team colors were seal brown and gold, not orange and blue.

The team wore the original seal brown and gold in 1960 and 1961, the first two seasons of play.

2. John Elway actually was not on scholarship his last two years at Stanford.

He had signed a minor league baseball contract with the Yankees, and college rules at that time were such that he had to relinquish his football scholarship. So John Elway actually had to pay his own way for his last two years of college.

1. Everybody knows it is hard to get a ticket to a Broncos home game.

But do you know when this sellout streak actually began? The last non-sellout was the final game of the 1969 season. The Broncos have been sold out for 39 straight years, including 2008.

Misses

10. Terry Pierce.
Second round, 2003, Kansas.

9. Allen Aldridge.
Second round, 1994, Houston.

8. Darius Watts.
Second round, 2004, Marshall.

7. Paul Toviessi.
Second round, 2001, Marshall.

6. Dan Williams.
First round, 1993, Toledo.

5. Mike Croel.
First round, Nebraska, 1991. One year and gone.

4. George Foster.
First round 2003, Georgia. Miscast as a tackle. Some teams had him going in third round. A major reach and even bigger bust.

3. Marcus Nash.
First round, 1998, Tennessee. SEC coaches were leery of this pick. Shanahan didn't listen.

2. Willie Middlebrooks.
First round, 2001, Minnesota. Never found a position or three healthy weeks in a row.

1. Ted Gregory.
First round, 1988, Syracuse. Shorter than Bob Knight's temper. Pocketed a half million and headed back east.

Hits

All should be in the Hall of Fame. None are.

5. Randy Gradishar.
First round, 1974.

4. Karl Mecklenburg.
12th round, 1983.

3. Steve Atwater.
First round, 1989.

2. Shannon Sharpe.
Seventh round, 1990.

1. Terrell Davis.
Seventh round, 1994.

First-Round Picks That Didn't Stick

The Denver Broncos have had six first-round draft picks since 2000. Only two have stuck around. For the record:

5. Deltha O'Neal.

The cornerback from the University of California, Berkeley, was the 15th pick overall in 2000. He lasted a couple of years and then they parted ways. Traded to Cincinnati. Except for Jay Cutler, O'Neal was the highest pick in the decade. Our verdict: Wasted pick.

4. Willie Middlebrooks.

The cornerback from Minnesota was the 24th pick overall in 2001. He played for David Gibbs in college and Gibbs pushed hard for him here. He had a bad knee and never earned a starting spot.

3. Ashley Lelie.

The wideout from Hawaii was selected number 19 in 2002. There were high hopes that he could stretch the defense with his speed. It ended badly with lots of hard feelings.

2. George Foster.

The offensive tackle from Georgia was number 20 in the first round in 2003. Biggest guy they ever drafted. He was so-so and Denver traded him to Detroit for Dre Bly.

1. DJ Williams and Jay Cutler.

The linebacker and a quarterback, respectively. Picks in 2004 and 2006. Both can play. Both are still in Denver. We'll see.

If you're a longtime Broncos fan, you've picked up a lot of information by osmosis over the years. People call this "trivia." We prefer to call it "relevant minutiae." Here's a list of anecdotes and factoids that Broncos fans should—and probably do—know. Listed in order of how important or well-known each item is in the larger universe of Broncos knowledge.

10. Nasty.

Tight-end-turned-wide-receiver Nate Jackson is a big music fan. He plays in a band under the stage name Jack Nasty.

9. Another QB from Stanford.

John Lynch, all-pro safety, played four seasons at Stanford—two at quarterback.

8. Hoops snapper.

Mike Leach, the Broncos long-snapper, went to Jefferson Township High School in Jefferson Township, NJ. He graduated as the school's all-time leading scorer in basketball.

7. Plot twist.

Former Broncos kicker Jason Elam wrote a novel, a religious thriller called Monday Night Jihad. Co-written with his pastor Steve Yohn, the story involves a horrific stadium bombing and a Christian football hero (a linebacker) who fights terrorism. There's also some humor and romance. We remain flabbergasted that the Broncos let Elam get away to Atlanta.

6. The Giants scandal.

The Broncos first head coach Frank Filchock played for the Giants back in the day. He was involved in scandal revolving around the Giants' 1946 NFL title game with the Chicago Bears. Hours before the game, the New York district attorney's office announced that Filchock and another player had been bribed with money and off-season jobs in exchange for a Chicago win. One Giants player confessed and was not allowed to play. Filchock denied it. He played hard, throwing two touchdown passes and suffering a broken nose. The Giants lost by 10. Both Giants players were absolved of criminal wrongdoing but were suspended indefinitely from NFL play. Filchock then played in Canada. He was reinstated by the NFL in 1950.

5. Rick Upchurch.

He's the Broncos' all-time record holder for punts returned and yards gained. He was the 1975 Rookie of the Year. Rick once dated Secretary of State Condoleezza Rice when she was a student at DU. Rick's stepdaughter, Stacie Lynn Jones, appeared on Donald Trump's The Apprentice TV show in 2004.

4. Last-minute QB.

In 1960 Denver was awarded an AFL franchise. Frank Filchock was head coach, and Frank Tripucka was an assistant. After one week of practice, Filchock realized he didn't have a quarterback. He asked Tripucka to come out of retirement. The former Notre Dame star had already played ten seasons in the NFL and Canadian football. It worked out pretty well for Tripucka. He threw the first touchdown pass in the history of the AFL. In 1962 he played in the All-Star game. He's fifth on the all-time franchise list for career passing. His number, 18, was *supposed* to be retired. But in 2005, it was discovered that his number had not been retired after all. Bonus trivia: The only two numbers retired by the Broncos are 44 (Floyd Little) and 7 (John Elway.)

3. A champ by any other name.

Champ Bailey was the State High Jump champ in Georgia. His mother gave him the nickname "Champ." His real name is Roland.

2. From QB to coach.

Head Coach Mike Shanahan was a quarterback Eastern Illinois University. He lost a kidney after taking a hard hit in practice. That ended his career as an athlete, and almost killed him. His son, Kyle Shanahan, is the Offensive Coordinator for the Houston Texans.

1. Three generations.

John Albert Elway, Jr. became the QB coach for Cherry Creek High School, where his son Jack (John Albert Elway III) was a star QB. Jack now plays for Arizona State. Jack Elway, Sr. was head coach at Stanford from 1984 to 1988.

Calling It Like I See It :: Jim Evans

Note: Jim Evans had a marvelous career as an umpire in the American League. Now retired, he runs a baseball school for umpires. He lives in Parker, Colorado. We asked him to list several of his "baseball bests."

Most Memorable Event: Introduction of Ted Williams.

Of all the games I worked in my 28 years as Major League umpire (including regular season, League Championships, World Series, no-hitters, and perfect games), the most memorable event for me was the introduction of Ted Williams at the 1999 All-Star Game in Boston. He was the last player introduced as MLB was naming the Team of the Century. The reception Ted received as he proceeded from centerfield to the mound in a golf cart was electrifying and something I will never forget. I was the plate umpire for this game and standing in front of the Boston dugout waiting for our TV cue before proceeding to home plate for the plate meeting and line-up card exchange. Ted's cart stopped directly in front of me as the PA announcer was enumerating Ted's career highlights. He reached out and shook hands with me. He recognized me but couldn't remember my name. My first year in the American League, Ted was the manager of the Texas Rangers. He said, "I remember you. You nearly threw my ass out of a game one night down in Texas. You told me to put my hands in my pockets while arguing. I never forgot that. That was good advice. You probably saved me a helluva lot of money!" Ted was then driven up onto the mound and All-Stars from both teams surrounded him and were reaching out and trying to touch him. There wasn't a dry eye among them, including me. The standing ovation from the fans went on forever. The pre-game went 20 minutes longer than the network had planned. As the plate umpire, I had to give the network an extra 30 seconds between half-innings for the first five innings to make-up for the commercials they missed. It was truly a night I will never forget. I don't remember much about the game, but the pre-game—that's something I will never forget.

Best Outfielder: Jim Edmonds.

In my opinion, the best outfielder I saw in my career was Jim Edmonds. He always made the routine play but got to balls that most Major League fielders would just try to cut-off. Taking nothing from the great Willie Mays, but I saw Edmonds make some catches that would make Willie's spectacular catch look routine. Bo Jackson made some of the most unbelievable plays I ever saw but he was not nearly as consistent as Edmonds. I saw Jackson throw a runner out at the plate from the warning track in left field when the runner was tagging and Jackson had climbed the wall to make the catch. It was a perfect one-hopper to the plate. The next inning, he dropped a pop-up with two outs that allowed two runs to score.

Best Clutch Hitter: Paul Molitor.

Paul Molitor was not only one of the best hitters of all time but, in my opinion, he was Mr. Clutch. He established a World Series record in one of the Series I worked in 1982, going 5 for 5. That didn't surprise me at all. He was the best I ever saw at coming through in pressure, game-winning situations.

Best Pitcher: Catfish Hunter.

Catfish Hunter gets my vote. I can't quote his stats but I can tell you that he took command when he entered the mound. He was fearless and challenged hitters. He gave up a lot of one-run homers but he never backed down. His greatest strength was his ability to spot the ball exactly where he wanted it. He spent the first two innings defining the umpire's strike zone and then could throw the pitch precisely where he wanted it the remainder of the game. He kept hitters off balance.

Most Intimidating Pitcher: Nolan Ryan.

Lots of opposing players developed "Ryanitis" on days Nolan was scheduled to pitch and took themselves out of the line-up for various reasons. Even though he was close to a .500 pitcher throughout his career, Nolan was a threat to throw a no-hitter every time he took the mound. I was the plate umpire for his first no-hitter in 1973. He holds the record with 7 no-hitters. And he came close several times with 10 or 12 one-hitters. Ryan was tough to catch, tough to hit, and tough to umpire. He threw over a 100 miles per hour at times and often had no idea where it was going. He kept everybody off balance. In ballparks where the shadows fell between home plate and the mound, Nolan was a serious health hazard. The closest second to Nolan and his intimidation factor I ever saw was Sam McDowell. I just caught him at the end of his career and he had lost lots of his velocity but still had lots of trouble finding the strike zone. There have been a lot of great closers who could throw extremely hard for an inning or two but it always amazed me that Nolan was often clocked just as fast in the ninth inning as he was in the first or second.

Best Catchers: Bob Boone and Ivan Rodriguez.

The best catcher I ever saw at handling pitchers and receiving pitches was Bob Boone. He was a master at setting-up and making pitches look good for his pitcher. He could frame pitches without jerking the mitt. He shifted his body almost imperceptibly and every pitch seemed to funnel in to him. The only way I figured out what he was doing was by studying him on video. The catcher with the best throwing arm I ever saw was Ivan Rodriguez. He had great arm strength but his biggest asset was his quickness. No lead was ever safe and he liked to throw behind runners. This means that the umpire, like the runners, had to be especially alert at all times. I've seen him pickoff runners who were looking right at him and no more than two or three steps off a base.

Toughest Call for Plate Umpire:

The steal of home. You have to be alert for a balk, batter interference, catcher interference, call the pitch, and call the play. This all occurs in about half a second and you have to maintain your position to call the pitch. You cannot adjust forward as the catcher does when he "reads" the steal. This means that on real close plays, you are looking through the catcher's back. It becomes an educated guess.

Another Tough Challenge:

Adjusting to a player's mistake. Umpiring is a matter of securing the perfect angle and distance for a particular play. After doing that, an umpire can then get blocked out because a player's mistake changes the development of the play.

Two of the most unusual things I have ever seen on a major league field:

2. Albert Belle broke his bat on a checked swing.

The bat actually broke in half and part of it ended up halfway to the mound. I called the pitch a ball.

1. Dave Kingman hit a high fly ball in the Metrodome in Minneapolis and the ball never came down.

It disappeared in one of the air vents in the secondary roof. Infielders and outfielders are converging to make the play and nothing comes down. I had to create a new ground rule on the spot. Ground rule double.

You've probably heard these names over the years. Then again, maybe you haven't. We're listing them here for posterity. All of these guys with local connections have made important contributions to sports and deserve a shout out.

10. Stan Albeck.

Coached the University of Denver basketball team in the mid 1960s. Then went to the Denver Rockets (1970-71.) Was the head coach at Cleveland (1979-80,) San Antonio (1980-83,) New Jersey Nets (1983-85) and Chicago Bulls (1985-86.)

9. Earl "Dutch" Clark.

Pueblo Central High School's star player in 1926. He led his basketball team to the state championship and to a second place finish in the national tournament. Many still think of him as the greatest athlete to ever come from a Colorado high school.

8. Carl Scheer.

Was hired in June of 1974 as the Nuggets' president and general manager. Scheer brought the 1984 NBA All-Star Game to McNichols Arena in Denver.

7. Jim Burris.

Managed the Denver Bears for 20 years. Longtime baseball reporter for *The Sporting News*.

6. Esfandiar "Esse" Baharmast.

Great soccer ref from Denver. He has officiated World Cup matches.

5. Don Hinchey.

University of Northern Colorado wrestler. Graduated in 1971. On the Denver Baseball Commission and the Denver Chamber of Commerce.

4. Fred Casotti.

A University of Colorado alum, he served in several capacities at CU—sports information director (1952-67,) assistant athletic director (1968-72) and associate athletic director (1973-85.)

3. Rich Clarkson.

Outstanding photographer. You've seen his work in *The Denver Post* and *Sports Illustrated*.

2. Roger Kinney.

A Denver native, he has long been a promoter of the city and local sports. He's involved with everything from the Colorado Sports Hall of Fame to junior golf to little league to the Chamber of Commerce. Helped bring the Final Four to Denver in 1990.

1. John Rayburn.

He was a popular local broadcaster with a 42-year career. His was a familiar face to almost everyone in Denver. Did great play-by-play broadcasts. He anchored the news on all three of Denver's network stations at one time or another.

Ten more:

10. Bill Reed.

He was the voice of the old Denver Bears. He was a snappy dresser. He would take off his pants during the broadcast so he didn't lose the crease. He worked the game in his shorts. It got awkward when a player's wife came up to the booth to do a promotion.

9. Chris Mueller.

From Germany. He played a lot of soccer and competed for the Denver Kickers. He was a bartender at the Old Park Lane Hotel. In 1965, he bought the Red Lion Restaurant, a Boulder landmark.

8. Dad Felix and Pop Daly.

They were local baseball heroes in the 1940s. They played on Sundays and their games drew big crowds. A guy would pass the hat in the crowd for beer money for the players. Lots of memories for old timers when you mention Felix and Daly.

7. Drew Litton.

Sports editorial cartoonist at the *Rocky Mountain News*.

6. Gene Hochevar.

Coached at Englewood High School. An assistant at CU working for Chuck Fairbanks. Gene is one of the founders of the American Football Alumni.

5. Fisher DeBerry.

Head coach at Air Force for 23 years. Only Joe Paterno and Bobby Bowden have longer tenures at one school.

4. Sonny Lubick.

Turned around CSU football.

3. Bob Blasi.

A coaching legend at the University of Northern Colorado.

2. Larry Varnell.

Played for the old Denver Nuggets after World War II. Then he coached Regis College basketball (The Buzz Boys) with great success. Later he became a successful basketball official.

1. George Ratterman.

He taught Joe Williams how to sell real estate. Irv Brown's sons Dave, Tim and Mark were in George's baseball school. George was one of the finest all-round athletes in Notre Dame history, playing football, basketball, baseball and tennis. He alternated at quarterback with Johnny Lujack on Notre Dame's 1946 team. He played for the Buffalo Bills and the New York Yanks, and was later a backup to the Cleveland Browns' Otto Graham. George was a pro football commentator in the 1960s and early 1970s for ABC and NBC. George was unique. He had a great sense of humor. In 1961 he was elected sheriff in Campbell County, Kentucky. He passed away in November 2007.

Colorado Avalanche players have shown this town what playoff hockey looks like, and there's no turning back. Here are our all-time favorite Avs.

5. Adam Foote.

1995-2004, 2008-current. Known for his warrior-mentality. A gritty player. Intense. His return to the Avs lineup has demonstrated how foolish it was to let him go in the first place. He's the heart and soul of this team.

4. Raymond Bourque.

1999-2001. His drive for the Stanley Cup inspired his team and this town. Hall of Famer Ray Bourque was key to the Stanley Cup Championship in 2001.

3. Peter Forsberg.

1995-2003, 2008-current. "Peter the Great." A real dazzler. Quick, skilled. A magician at times. Tough, too. He doesn't back down.

2. Patrick Roy.

1995-2003. The very definition of a competitor. Ferocious. The NHL's all-time winingest goaltender.

1. Joe Sakic.

1995-current. One of the most beloved athletes ever to play in Denver. Super Joe. A quality guy. He comes through in the clutch. Best hands in town.

My Top Ten Denver Sports Highlights
:: Adam Cayton-Holland

Note: Denver native and stand-up comedian Adam Cayton-Holland writes a column for *Westword*.

10. 1986, 1987, 1989, the Denver Broncos lose three Super Bowls, two consecutively, by a combined total of 136–40.

John Elway is at the helm of all three failed efforts and children of the Rocky Mountain region are forced to deal with the reality that their hero, their god, while amazing, is viewed by the national media as incapable of winning a national championship. Doubts are sown deep into these children, grave concerns about heroes, mortality, the validity of their city. While this may not seem like a sports highlight, it is crucial in Denver lore to understand the pathos it takes to make victory in true sports towns so sweet.

9. 1993, on his birthday, a 13-year-old Adam Cayton-Holland throws out opening pitch at a Denver Zephyrs game.

Little guy smokes heat down the center of the plate. "Sign that kid up," someone yells from the stands. And that someone is right.

8. 2004, Lakewood, Rockies' pitcher Denny Neagle is caught with a prostitute in his car who is later revealed to be the inspiration for the orcs in Peter Jackson's adaptation of *The Lord of the Rings*.

The Rockies unceremoniously can their botched five-year, $51 million dollar experiment and begin to refocus the franchise on cultivating young talent, not buying it for egregious sums. This pays off huge later.

7. 1994, Miracle in Michigan.

Down 26-21 to the Michigan Wolverines with six seconds remaining in the game, the Colorado Golden Buffaloes' quarterback Kordell Stewart chucks the ball over 70 yards into the end-zone, where it is deflected by a Michigan player and then caught by Michael Westbrook in what is one of the wildest finishes in the history of college football. The program celebrates the victory but eventually disintegrates into nothing more than a thinly veiled excuse for date rape. Sad, sad.

6. 1987, Washington Park, Denver.

Rec-soccer titans the City Park Starchasers discover that cluster-fuck soccer may not be the best way to play when nubile, long-locked forward Adam Cayton-Holland finds net for the first time in his life. He likes the taste so much he goes on to score twice more that game, completing the hat trick. In the mid-90s the legendary footballer excites Colorado sports-enthusiasts yet again by perfecting the goal dance.

5. 2007, Todd Helton hits a walk-off homerun to win the second game of a doubleheader against the Los Angeles Dodgers.

The shot keeps the Colorado Rockies hopes alive for a wild-card berth and comes to define the beginning of their remarkable late-season tear, the same tear that earned the team their first pennant which couldn't have happened if Denny Neagle wasn't so fond of ugly blow-jobs. Rounding the bases, Helton is overcome with emotion, tosses his helmet into the air and dives into the arms of his teammates waiting for him at home plate. For the first time in his career, Helton lets down his poker face and we see how badly this guy wants it.

4. 1994, Eighth Seed Denver Nuggets Defeat the First Seed Seattle Supersonics.

The first time such an upset occurs in NBA Playoffs history, star center Dikembe Mutombo celebrates by grabbing the ball and collapsing to the floor in joy, screaming in a variety of languages, none of them intelligible.

3. 1992, Catholic Youth Recreation Association Summer Baseball League.

En-route to a championship season (later revoked for unequal distribution of playing time—against league policy, the fuckers), the Jayhawks are tied with the Mother of God Stars. Star shortstop Adam Cayton-Holland is the runner on first base, the bases are loaded, two outs, two balls, two strikes. The first-base coach instructs Adam to run on anything, advice he takes quite literally. So much so that when the opposing pitcher proceeds to throw ball three, Adam takes off. Utter chaos ensues, as all three runners sprint back-and-forth, back-and-forth between bases as the Stars try to get them out. Ultimately the ball is misplayed (we were twelve) and the runners advance, bringing home a run. Everyone marvels at Cayton-Holland's run-producing ingenuity in a play that everyone who's anyone in Denver considers top three all-time.

2. 2007, One Game Playoff between the Colorado Rockies and the San Diego Padres, 163rd Game of the Regular Season.

After a nail-biting four-hours-and-change of battle, the Padres take an 8-6 lead in the top of the 13th then send stud-reliever Trevor Hoffman in to finish us off. The remarkable 13 out of 14 season-ending run that got the Rockies to this game in the first place appears to be over. Then Kazuo Matsui slaps a double. Then Troy Tulowitzki does the same, bringing Matsui home. Then Matt Holliday smashes a triple, tying the score. Hoffman walks Helton to face Jamey Carroll who promptly lines to right field. Holliday tags up. The throw comes into the plate. The catcher drops the ball. Holliday slides head-first. Does he tag the plate? Is he out? The umpire calls him safe! The Rockies are in the playoffs! The Rockies are in the playoffs! I am at the game and immediately deem it the singular greatest sports moment I have ever witnessed live. The only reason this is not number one is because Elway has to be, otherwise I would not be a Denverite. It is maybe the best night of my life.

1. 1998, Super Bowl XXXII, Denver vs. Green Bay.

Third down play, third quarter, John Elway runs for eight yards before leaping for the first down. While still in the air he's lambasted by two Packers, helicopter-spinning him so that he winds up facing the end-zone with the first down. While other mere mortals would have crumbled into dust, Elway survives. The Broncos go on to win their first Super Bowl ever and the play comes to symbolize the hunger, drive and determination of #7, the very same passion that Denver witnessed for years but never to ultimate success. The suffering ends. The doubt ends. The "Yeah, but can he win the big one" talk ends. The greatest quarterback of all time has his ring. The city is validated. My friends and I decide we must destroy it. We head downtown to riot and we honk the horn of my friend's old Volvo the entire time, prompting this comment from a passer-by, "Sounds like your horn needs a cough drop!" It is maybe the best night of my life.

Most Astonishing Series of One-Game Performances by Denver Pros

Denver fans have witnessed many a jaw-dropping heart-stopper. Who can forget "The Dive" (not to be confused with "The Drive")—John Elway's successful plunge for a first down in the Super Bowl against Green Bay—he spun in midair like a helicopter blade. That qualifies as astonishing. Here are ten performances that rate as all-time marvels.

10. 1987 AFC Championship game.
Denver beat Houston 38-33. A wild one that was finally decided by Jeremiah Castillo recovering a fumble on the three-yard line with one minute left in the game.

9. 1993-94, Nuggets vs. Seattle.
The Denver Nuggets went 42-40, seeded 8th, playing No. 1 Seattle. Nuggets won the series three games to two—the last one on the road in Seattle in overtime. Mahmoud Abdul Raul was the scoring leader. Dikembe Mutombo was a monster on the board.

8. 1996 Avs win the Stanley Cup.
The Avalanche swept Florida four games to none. Joe Sakic had 18 playoff goals, scored 34 points and had six game winning goals.

7. December 13, 1984, the highest-scoring game in NBA history.
Detroit beat Denver 186 to 184 in triple overtime. Four guys scored over 40 points: John Long had 41 and Isaiah Thomas had 47 for the Pistons. Alex English had 47 and Kiki Vandeweghe had 51 for the Nuggets.

6. 1998 Super Bowl XXXIII.
Denver beat Atlanta 34-19. John Elway was the MVP and threw for 336 yards—third most in Super Bowl history. He also ran for a three-yard score, making him the oldest player—at the ripe old age of 38—to score a touchdown in a Super Bowl.

5. 1997 Super Bowl XXXII.
Denver, a 13-point underdog, beat Green Bay 31-24. Terrell Davis had a great year. He rushed for 1,750 yards and had 15 TDs. He was sensational in the Bowl despite a migraine. A migraine! He was named MVP.

4. April 9, 1978, most one-game points scored by a Nugget.
The Nuggets' David Thompson scored 73 vs. Detroit. Later in the same game, the Iceman George Gervin scored 63 to win the ABA season scoring title by a tiny margin.

3. September 18, 2007, Rockies vs. Dodgers.
Todd Helton's two-out, two-strike walk-off homerun in the ninth inning propelled the Rockies to win 21 of their 22-game winning streak. It kept the Rockies alive for the wild card bid, and they went on to World Series.

2. April 9, 1993, Rockies Opening Day.
The Rockies host Montreal at Mile High Stadium. Eric Young homers to lead off the first inning in front of 80,227 fans.

1. 1986 AFC Championship game.

"The Drive." Cleveland. Wind chill minus 5 degrees. The Broncos down 20-13 to with 5:43 left in the game. The ball on the two-yard line. John Elway led a clutch drive that culminated with a pass to Mark Jackson with 37 seconds left to tie it up. Denver won in overtime on a Rich Karlis field goal.

Pro football often dominates the discussion on our radio show. No matter the season, there's always something to say about the Broncos. But we strive for variety. Here are 15 local sports highlights that have nothing to do with Broncos football.

15. First Rockies Postseason.
On October 3, 1995, the Rockies lost to Atlanta in their first-ever postseason appearance. Still, it was the postseason. That's something.

14. College hoops.
In 1990, Denver hosted the Final Four. UNLV beat Duke.

13. Rugby comes to Glendale.
Infinity Park, just outside Denver, is the nation's first municipal rugby stadium, seating 5,000 fans. Local men's, women's and youth teams are starting to popularize this fast, rough, demanding (yet surprisingly civil) sport in a town that just can't get enough sports.

12. Colorado Rapids Soccer.
In 2007, the team and a growing number of fans inaugurated Dick's Sporting Goods Park. Not a lot of big wins yet, but a lot of heart.

11. Rulon wins gold.
Rulon Gardner, the literally death-defying amateur wrestler from Wyoming (and a resident of Colorado Springs) won gold in the Sydney Olympics in an amazing upset of the Russian three-time gold-medal winner, Alexander Karelin.

10. Another sweet upset.
In 2001, the CU Buffs stunned the Nebraska Cornhuskers in Boulder, stomping 'em with a 62 to 36 victory.

9. Falcons beat the Irish.
In 1985, for the fourth consecutive time, Air Force football defeated Notre Dame. The Falcons blocked a field goal, returned it for a TD and won 21-15.

8. Tulo's Triple Play.
On April 29, 2007, Rockies rookie shortstop Troy Tulowitzki became the 13th player in MLB history to turn an unassisted triple play. Tulo caught a line drive, stepped on second, tagged a runner and threw to first for good measure. Kid has talent.

7. ABA Finals.
After winning 60 games in the 1975-76 season, the Nuggets faced Dr. J and the New York Nets in the ABA finals. Nets won.

6. CU Skiers.

The University of Colorado Ski Team has won 16 national championships since 1954, when the NCAA first sanctioned skiing.

5. DU Skiers.

The Denver Pioneers Ski Team has won 19 NCAA championships. In 2008, they were underdogs, battling injuries and illness. They were expected to finish fourth, but they pulled off another win. DU has won the title five times since 2000.

4. Colorado Mammoth Lacrosse.

More than a million fans came out to cheer during the 2006 season, when the Mammoth won the Champion's Cup.

3. Colorado Crush Arena Football.

John Elway is Crush co-owner and CEO. In 2005, the Crush beat the Georgia Force to win the league championship in ArenaBowl XIX.

2. Buffs beat the Irish.

In the Orange Bowl, 1991. CU shared the national championship with Georgia Tech.

1. All-Star Basketball.

The Nuggets have yet to win a championship. But this town has seen some great basketball. Denver hosted the NBA All-Star Games 1984 and 2005. The 1976 ABA All-Star Game turned into the first slam-dunk contest, converting many in Denver to basketball fanhood. Julius Erving versus David Thompson. The Nuggets won it, 144-138.

Five Nuggets for All Time :: Nick Sclafani

Note: Nick Sclafani, publisher of *The Nugg Doctor* at www.nuggdoctor.blogspot.com, is an alumnus of Colorado State University. *The Nugg Doctor* blog was created in February of 2006 and has been featured in *SLAM* magazine, *Dime* magazine, and on ESPN. He lists his top Nuggets of all time.

5. Dikembe Mutombo.

Mt. Mutombo was selected fourth overall by the Denver Nuggets in the 1991 NBA Draft. As a rookie, he was selected for the All-Star team by averaging 16.6 points, 12.3 rebounds, and nearly three blocks per game. In Mutombo's third season, Denver pulled off a major playoff upset by stunning the top-seeded Seattle Supersonics in the first round—the first eighth seed to win an NBA playoff series. At the end of Game 5 Mutombo fell to the ground, clutching the ball. It's a scene engraved in the memory of every Nuggets fan. While a Nugget, Dikembe was the NBA Defensive Player of the Year in 1995, and was an All-Star in 1992, 1995, and 1996. There has never been better shot blocker. Mt. Mutombo is the franchise leader in blocked shots (1,486), average blocked shots (3.81), most blocks in a season (4.49), and most blocked shots in a single game (12). And as a rebounder, he makes a pretty strong case too, holding the single season rebounding record (1,070), career highest rebound average (12.3), most rebounds in a single game (31), and the highest rebounding average per game for a season (13.0) in Nuggets' franchise history.

4. Byron Beck.

He was the first player signed by the original Denver Rockets franchise in 1967 and fittingly, his number, 40, was the first to be retired by the Nuggets. The two-time ABA All-Star stands in fifth place on the Nuggets all-time scoring list (8,603), second in rebounds (5,621), and third in games played (747). In the 1973 ABA Playoffs, Beck averaged nearly 20 points per game. And in 1976, he helped lead the Nuggets to the ABA Finals.

3. David Thompson.

The one they called "Sky Walker." One of the greatest scorers and leapers of all-time. In his seven seasons, Thompson racked up 11,992 points (third all-time)—many of which were accompanied by awe-inspiring aerial display. DT holds the third highest franchise points-per-game average (24.1) and scored an incredible franchise record of 73 points in one game which is the second most scored by a player in a non-overtime game in NBA history. All-NBA First Team in 1977 and 1978, he made three-straight All-Star appearances, earning MVP honors in the 1979 contest. He's also only player to be named the MVP in both an ABA and NBA All-Star game. David, a truly unique talent, was inducted in the Hall of Fame in 1996. His number, 33, has since been retired.

2. Dan Issel.

"The Horse" was as steady as could be. Issel played in 1,218 of 1,242 possible games for Denver while holding the franchise records for career rebounds (6,630) and personal fouls (2,304.) He ranks second in career scoring (16,589), minutes (25,200), and is tied with two others for most seasons as a Nugget (10). He trails only Kareem Abdul-Jabbar, Wilt Chamberlain, Julius Erving, Moses Malone, Michael Jordan and Karl Malone in combined ABA/NBA scoring. "The Horse," a 1976 ABA All-Star and 1977 NBA All-Star, became the first Nugget to be elected to the Hall of Fame in 1993. His number, 44, has since been retired.

1. Alex English.

Simply stated: English scored more points in the decade of the 1980s than any other NBA player and he did so as a Nugget. A second-team All-NBA member in 1982, 1983 and 1986, English guided the Nuggets to Division championships in 1984-85 and 1987-88. He is the All-Time leader in franchise history in the following categories: most seasons (11), career games (837), consecutive games (387), minutes (29,893), points scored (21,645), career average ppg (25.9), most seasons scoring 2,000+ points (8), career most 40-point games (34), 50-point games (2), and 30-point games in a career (268). He led the league in scoring in 1982-83 with a scoring average of 28.4 points and also set the franchise single season scoring record three years later at 29.8 points per game. English was inducted into the Hall of Fame as a player in 1997. His number, 2, has since been retired.

Here are six teams that have come and gone from the Mile High city.

6. Denver Dynamos.

OK, they weren't so great. A franchise of the North American Soccer League from 1974 to 1975, this club never made it out of the league's basement. The franchise moved to Minnesota in 1975. Time to take the faded blue Dynamos pennant off the wall, kids. But we'll never forget the goofy logo: A lower-case "d" for Denver with a soccer ball in the center. The Seventies will never die.

5. Colorado Xplosion.

Colorado's first professional women's basketball team, founded in 1996, won the Western Conference title of the American Basketball League in 1997. Team stars included Crystal Robinson, Tari Phillips and li'l Debbie Black. Black was the first woman in pro basketball to score a Quadruple Double: 10 points, 14 rebounds, 12 assists and 10 steals against Atlanta in 1996. The ABL melted down during the 1998-99 season, and the Colorado Xplosion "implosioned."

4. Denver Racquets.

Denver's team won the first-ever championship of World Team Tennis in 1974, defeating Billie Jean King's team, Philadelphia Freedom. Then the Racquets promptly moved to Phoenix. Love all.

3. Colorado Chill.

Our second professional women's basketball team was a winner. The Chill played in the National Women's Basketball League, racking up back-to-back championship titles in 2005 and 2006. The league folded in 2007. Chill stars—including Becky Hammon, Ruth Riley and Katie Cronin—also played in the Women's National Basketball League. Efforts have been made to revive the Chill as a WNBA franchise. At this point, it looks like it's not gonna happen.

2. Denver Bears.

A sentimental favorite for many Denver baseball fans. Originally, they played at Merchants Park at Broadway and Exposition, but that was little more than a dirt lot. In the late 1940s the city offered a plot of land at Federal and 17th where a new ballpark was built. It became known as Bears Stadium. The stadium got rave reviews because it was designed to take advantage of the hill right there—the stands were supported by the hill, so there were no poles or girders. All fans had a clear view of the field. This "baseball amphitheater" was considered a postwar marvel. In 1951, half a million fans attended games at Bears Stadium. In the mid-50s, the dream of attracting a MLB franchise took over. It's a long story but Broncos football emerged out of all that, and Bear Stadium was expanded to accommodate the new team. In the mid-1980s the Bears became the Zephyrs, named after the Greek god of wind, or a passenger train, depending on who you ask. When the Rockies came to Denver in 1993, the Zephyrs moved to New Orleans. A lot of great memories were made at Bears Stadium. Bears Woody Held, Tony Kubek, Bobby Richardson and Marv Thornberry all made it to the Bigs.

1. Denver Gold.

For a minute it looked as if Denver might be able to support two pro football teams. From 1983 to 1985 the Denver Gold, a franchise of the United States Football League, was a leader in fan attendance. Former Broncos Head Coach Red Miller was the Gold's first coach, followed by former Broncos QB Craig Morton. When the league switched to a fall schedule, fans weren't happy about the Gold "competing" with the Broncos for fan support. The Gold and the league soon folded.

Top Colorado Pitchers

These are the best pitchers from Colorado, not best Colorado Rockies pitchers.

6. Dennis Rasmussen.
Bear Creek. Played for years with several teams.

5. Tippy Martinez.
LaJunta. Great years with Baltimore, out of the Bullpen.

4. Danny Jackson.
Aurora Central. A star with Cincinnati and Kansas City.

3. Stan Williams.
East. Won 102 games with the Dodgers on a staff with Sandy Koufax, Don Drysdale and Johnny Podres.

2. Goose Gossage.
Wasson High. Inducted into the Hall of Fame in 2008.

1. Roy Halladay.
The best pitcher from Metro Denver. He played for Jim Capra at Arvada West. He's one of the top pitchers in the Big Leagues, period. Won the Cy Young Award in 2003. His record is 22 and seven. At this writing his overall is 105 and 52. An overpowering man with great size—six-foot-six, 275 pounds.

Five Toughest Hitters :: Goose Gossage

Note: Rich "Goose" Gossage grew up in Colorado Springs and went to Wasson High School. He and his wife still live in the Springs. He was one of the greatest relief pitchers ever. Goose was a closer. He played 21 seasons with nine teams, most notably the New York Yankees and San Diego Padres. He pitched in three World Series. Goose was finally elected to the Hall of Fame in 2008 and was the only player to be inducted in the class of 2008. He wrote his autobiography in 2000, entitled *The Goose Is Loose*. He got his nickname in 1972 when one of his teammates said he looked like a goose when he leaned in to look at the catcher. We asked Goose to name the five toughest hitters he faced in his career.

5. Al Kaline. Clutch guy.
All line drives.

4. Richie Zisk.
Pitch him in he'd kill you. Could really go the opposite way.

3. Dick Allen.
Great wrists. Phenomenal what he did in 1972 when he was the MVP.

2. Tony Olivo.
Pure hitter like Brett. If he could run, his average would have been much higher.

1. George Brett.
Pure. Did whatever the team needed. He was a double machine.

Five Favorite Pitchers :: Bus Campbell

Note: In February 2008, we lost Colorado Sports Hall of Famer and pitching guru, Robert "Bus" Campbell. He spent most of his 87 years helping Colorado pitchers succeed in the majors. Bus graduated from Manual High School in 1939. He was in the Coast Guard for a time then came back to Denver and became a teacher, teaching physical education in the Denver schools. Bus was the pitching coach at CU when Irv coached the Buffs.

Bus was a great coach—he kept it all so simple. He knew how to recognize talent and how to develop it. Everything he did to help pitchers, he did out of love for the game. Bus also coached at Iowa and was a scout for the Cardinals, Reds, Royals and Blue Jays. As one of the premier pitching coaches in America, he worked with 65 Big Leaguers. Over the years, his students included Jay Howell, Nick Willhite, Goose Gossage, Brad Lidge, Shawn Chacon, Mark Huismann, Scott Elarton, Brian Fisher, Bob Welch, Danny Jackson, Mike Trujillo, Darrel Akerfelds, Clint Zavaras and Cal Eldred. We'll miss you, Bus.

Before he passed away, we asked Bus to name his five top "students." This is what he said:

5. George Frazier.
Re-fixed his pitches when he was with the Boulder Collegians. He played for the Cardinals, Yankees, Indians, Cubs and Twins. He's now a commentator for the Rockies.

4. Mark Knudson.
Got him to use his legs more. He made the most improvement. He played for the Astros, Brewers and, very briefly, the Rockies.

3. Roy Halladay.
Gave him the knuckle curve, which is still his best pitch. Roy was the 2003 AL Cy Young Award winner.

2. Burt Hooton.
Worked with him on the knuckle curve, his signature pitch. He pitched for the Cubs, Dodgers and Rangers.

1. Jamie Moyer.
Helped him change his delivery and had him rely less on his fastball. He has 2,125 career strikeouts as of this writing. A star with the Mariners from 1996-2006, he's now with the Phillies—at age 45.

Best All-Around Baseball Players :: Tony DeMarco

Note: Tony DeMarco is a veteran baseball writer. He worked at the *Miami Herald* from 1981 to 1987, *Fort Worth Star-Telegram* from 1987 to 1994, *The Denver Post* from 1994 to 2000, and MSNBC 2000-present. He lives in Denver. Tony lists the five best all-around players in order.

5. George Brett.
A great stroke who flirted with 400 late in the season.

4. Ken Griffey, Jr.
Before the injuries he was the best all-around player in the game.

3. Alex Rodriguez.
If he stays at shortstop he's the greatest ever at the position. He could break Bonds' homerun mark.

2. Barry Bonds.
Forget the steroids. He still has the sweetest stroke in the game.

1. Larry Walker.
One of the few five-tool players in the game.

Bauldie Moschetti and the Boulder Collegians

Colorful baseball coach Bauldie Moschetti is in the Colorado Sports Hall of Fame. He recruited many great college players to come to Boulder and play for his semipro Boulder Collegians. Bauldie established the team in 1964, and it became one of the best semipro teams in the country. The Collegians won four National Baseball Congress National Championships, in 1966, 1967, 1975 and 1978. Joe Carter, Bob Welch, Tony Gwynn and Jay Howell all played for Bauldie. Two of his best pitchers went on to star in the World Series.

Baseball was Bauldie's passion. He always wore his black windbreaker no matter the temperature, and he always scribbled his lineups on old cigarette cartons, which drove the umpires nuts. Bus Campbell was the pitching coach for the Collegians, where he taught future Big League pitchers such as Steve Busby and Mark Langston. The team's last season was 1980. Bauldie had 112 players who went into pro baseball. In our opinion, these were the top five Collegians:

5. Roy Smalley.
From a very athletic family. Played in the Bigs with Minnesota, Texas and the Yankees. He was drafted five times before he signed with Texas.

4. Larry Gura.
Bauldie got him from Arizona State. He pitched 14 years for the Cubs, Royals, and Yankees.

3. Dick Ruthven.
Had those good years with the Cubs.

2. Burt Hooten.
Had the best knuckle curve we've ever seen. Many tried to copy it. Few succeeded.

1. Bob Horner.
The scariest right-handed hitter ever. You didn't want to be playing third when he was up. He would have been terrifying with an aluminum bat.

Great players who played in the National Baseball Congress:

6. Satchel Paige.
Pitched in the first NBC tournament in 1935 and returned 25 years later to pitch for the Weller Indians from Wichita.

5. Don Sutton.
The Hall of Famer pitched for Wyoming and Michigan.

4. Ozzie Smith.
Was playing college ball at Cal Poly San Luis Obispo. Played for Clarinda, Iowa.

3. Whitey Herzog.
Played for the Springfield Illinois Generals.

2. Tom Seaver.
Played for the Alaska Gold Panners.

1. Ralph Houk.
Played for Fort Leavenworth, Kansas when he was stationed there in 1942.

You look like you could use some wholesome nostalgia. Did we ever tell you about the Denver Bears? Before we got a Major League franchise in the 1990s, this was a great Minor League town with the very popular Bears. They played Class A ball in the Western League at an all-dirt ballpark on South Broadway called Merchants Park. It was probably the worst field a professional team ever played on. Because there was no grass, a routine ground ball might go all the way to the wall. A kid never had to pay to get in. You'd just walk around until you found a hole in the grandstand and sneak in.

Back in the day, The *Denver Post* sponsored an annual tournament that drew players like Babe Ruth and Satchel Paige. It was a great era. Every Sunday a doubleheader: two seven-inning games and they didn't clear the park between games. Gamblers sat on the third base line and bet on everything. After World War II, there were great rivalries. The Lincoln Athletics featuring Nellie Fox and Bobby Shantz were a team to beat. Sioux City had Sam Brewer. Des Moines had Stan Hack. Colorado Springs had Fat Pat Seerey. Pueblo had Danny Holden. One time, the Bears won 17 in a row and trainer Bill Behm wore the same white t-shirt and didn't wash it. It soon became a black shirt. It seemed like the same two guys umpired every game: Joe "Onions" Cibulka and Bob Phillips.

Two of the early managers were Mike Gazella and Andy Cohen. After pro ball, Andy went home to El Paso and coached UTEP. Irv's very first game as a coach at CU was against Andy and UTEP. Here are our favorite Denver Bears Class-A players.

10. Willie Skeen.
Local hero. Went to North High School. He always hit for a high average.

9. Bud Berinahele.
The smoothest first baseman. Made everything look easy. Line drive singles hitter.

8. Jack Whisenant.
Star football player at Michigan. Could turn the dp and was a gap hitter.

7. Fritz Brickell.
Energetic shortstop who made it to the Big Leagues. Irv worked with him at baseball camp. A great guy.

6. Warren "Cowboy" Martin.
The best stuff of anybody in the early days. Couldn't throw it over the plate.

5. Joe King.
Power hitter who started his hands up high like Yaz. Could really turn on the fastball.

4. Billy Bruton.
The centerfielder could run and hit. When he got to the Bigs with the Braves, he excelled.

3. Curtis Roberts.

A small second baseman who was a fan favorite. Great hustle.

2. Bill Pinckard.

Had amazing power. When they moved in the late 40s to Bears Stadium, he played Pepper off the old Coors building across the street from the park.

1. Chuck Tanner.

Became a Big League Manager. Was a terrific left-handed hitter. Big chew of tobacco. He rolled his knee for timing and hit nothing but line drives.

Our Favorite Billy Martin Quotes

Billy Martin is known for managing the New York Yankees and arguing with umpires. He managed the AAA Denver Bears for the last half of the 1968 season. He was never at a loss for words. Here are our favorite Billy Martin quotes.

6.
"All I know is, I pass people on the street and they don't know whether to say hello or goodbye."

5.
As a second-baseman-turned-manager advising his infielders how to protect themselves around the keystone sack: "If they try to knock you over, hit the [bleep] right in the mouth with the ball."

4.
Talking about Reggie Jackson and George Steinbrenner: "One is a born liar and the other is convicted."

3.
"When I get through managing I'm going to open a Kindergarten."

2.
"If there is such a thing as a good loser, then the game is crooked."

1.
"I didn't throw the first punch. I threw the second four."

Note: Dick Balderson has been in baseball for 40 years. After eight years as a player in the Minor Leagues, he went into player personnel. He joined the Rockies in their inaugural year and stayed seven years. Now he is a full time scout for the Atlanta Braves. Dick lists the top five scouts in his opinion.

5. Bus Campbell.
The premier pitching coach from Colorado who scouted very effectively for several teams.

4. Moose Johnson.
Lives in Denver, scouted for Toronto and Philly. Hard worker who could really spot talent.

3. Hugh Alexander.
Philadelphia. A great storyteller. Lost an arm in an accident and had to walk five miles to a hospital.

2. Tom Ferrick.
Another KC scout who lived in Philly. Everyone trusted him.

1. Rosey Gilhausen.
From Kansas City. He was an old timer who would get in the car and drive everywhere. There were no combines then. You did it all.

Note: Until 1997, baseball was the oldest sport played at the University of Denver. Pioneer Baseball had a 127-year run. Jack Rose was the most successful coach in school history. He coached 36 years and won 785 games. We asked Jack to list his best ten players.

10. Willie Sanchez.
Was a smooth outfielder who played pro ball and became a scout.

9. Paul Epperson.
From Littleton High School. Really utilized a big curve ball to be a big winner for DU.

8. Jim Elliott.
Was an All-American catcher in 1987. A great handler of pitchers.

7. Blazer McClure.
From Cherry Creek was the leader of the 1981 team that went 40-11.

6. Dave Black.
From Thomas Jefferson. Set a record for homeruns with 111.

5. Tim Waner.
A smooth third baseman from La Junta. He played pro ball. His daughter, Abby, is a star on Duke's women's basketball team.

4. Bob Fitzner.
A catcher who could really catch and throw. He played pro ball.

3. Jerry Causey.
A big first baseman who came to DU to play baseball. He played pro ball for the Astros. A power-hitting first baseman.

2. Steve Blateric.
From Lincoln High School. Jack's first recruit. He played major league baseball one year for the Red Sox.

1. Dan Schatzeder.
A left-handed pitcher who was in the Big Leagues for 15 years. He could swing the bat, too. He won a World Series game for the Minnesota Twins.

Our All-Time Top 50 Pros

No book like this would be complete without our listing the greatest local pros ever. There is no minimum on how many years they played. If we liked them, they are listed.

50. Greg Kragen.

Played nine years with the Broncos. He got cut the first time around but never gave up and ended up being in the Pro Bowl at nose guard.

49. Mark Schlereth.

Nobody was tougher. Nobody had more surgeries. What a great career at ESPN and now he's a detective on a soap opera.

48. Steve Sewell.

The guy from Oklahoma was the ultimate all-purpose back; and what a personality—just a pleasure to be around.

47. Tom Jackson.

When we first got him we thought he hurt his knee. It happened at the University of Louisville and he was solid here.

46. Jim Turner.

Old "High Tops" was very clutch. Will anyone ever forget the touchdown pass he caught, and that lumbering gait down the left sideline?

45. Troy Tulowitzki.

Yes we know he's just a rookie, but he's going to be in the Hall one day. Nobody, nobody goes in the hole and makes the long haul and throws like him. He's a good hitter who's going to just get better.

44. Barry Beck.

The best player on our first NHL team, the Rockies. A great fighter. When the club traded him, Joe Williams was a caller at the time, and was so upset he didn't renew his season tickets.

43. Rich Jackson.

The "Sheriff". He could rush the passer. Is in the Ring of Fame. Combined speed and toughness. Strong hands and he used them effectively to control the tackle blocking him.

42. Jeff Francis.

This smooth lefty looks like he's 16 years old. He won 17 games in the World Series year to tie Pedro Astacio and Kevin Ritz for the most wins in Rockies history.

41. Ellis Burks.

One of Don Baylor's favorites. Quiet, showed up to play everyday. Part of the Blake Street Bombers. A true pro.

40. LaPhonso Ellis.
He was a big factor when No. 1 Seattle lost to No. 8 Denver. He was a big help to Mutombo on the boards and was a clutch shooter.

39. Frank Tripucka.
He was going to coach for Frank Filchock in 1960, the Broncos first year. Frank had played for Filchock in Canada and was retired. That first camp was at Colorado School of Mines in Golden. Tripucka had something left and was an All-Star and is in the Ring of Fame.

38. Walter Davis.
Nobody could shoot the short jumper from the corner like "The Greyhound." He did it for Dean Smith at North Carolina and John McLoud with Phoenix. We got him at the tall end and he could still fill it up.

37. Dante Bichette.
When he was picked up in the expansion draft from Milwaukee, he was known as a defensive guy who had 12 kills. He was also known as a guy whose bat went cold when they came North from spring training. Here he hit a lot of homeruns and his fielding was left for the State Department.

36. Fat Lever.
Denver Nuggets. The best six-foot-three rebounder in the NBA. Led Denver in boards. He just timed everything. Wasn't too shabby on offense.

35. Marcus Camby.
He was the defensive player of the year in 2006. Great shot blocker who has stayed pretty healthy since coming here from the Knicks.

34. Steve Atwater.
The best hit ever at Mile High was Atwater nailing Christian Okoye.

33. John Lynch.
He really understands the game. Hard hitter, he'll punch your ticket. We love it when they play eight in the box and he blitzes.

32. Craig Morton.
When we got him from Dallas he was great. He led the team to its first Super Bowl. Craig was a pretty good baseball player at Cal. He played one summer with the Grand Junction Eagles.

31. Vinny Castilla.
The best pair of wrists to ever hit this town. The first year he'd only hit to dead center. As soon as he started pulling the ball he'd hit it out of the park. Outstanding on defense.

30. Dikembe Mutombo.
The best shot blocker ever. Better than McHale, Russell or Camby. Has the greatest timing ever. Not much on offense unless it was a stickback.

29. Calvin Natt.

Denver Nuggets. We got him from Portland and he was a man underneath. He was about six-foot-four but he backed down from no one.

28. Rod Smith.

This free agent has been a great wideout and go to guy for a long time. He was a quarterback at Missouri Southern.

27. Louie Wright.

A great cover corner who would tackle. He is so good with kids and coached high school football at Montbello. Now a physical ed teacher in Aurora.

26. Allen Iverson.

Great penetration, always at the free throw line. Andre Miller for A.I. was a steal. He and Melo could really do some damage.

25. Rob Blake.

Colorado Avalanche. Rugged guy who gave the club a real physical presence.

24. Karl Mecklenburg.

The best 12th round pick ever. He played on a bad Minnesota gopher team that was always behind in the fourth quarter. So the opponent never threw the ball and you couldn't grade his pass rush. He was like Randy White, never took a play off.

23. Billy Thompson.

A great safety who could really tackle. He wasn't too shabby returning punts.

22. Champ Bailey.

We got him from Washington for Clinton Portis. Has amazing skills, particularly if he has to catch up.

21. Jason Elam.

He has made so many clutch kicks and its effortless—he barely swings his leg.

20. Gary Zimmerman.

A great tackle that spent many years with the Vikings. He was a great left tackle who protected Elway's blind side.

19. Tom Nalen.

The best center Mike Shanahan has ever seen. Was drafted in the 7th round, 218th overall. He has been the key to Denver's rushing game.

18. Kiki Vandeweghe.

Nobody had a better first step. He'd look at his opponents' feet then pop a jumper. His dad Ernie was a star with the Knicks.

17. Floyd Little.

No. 44 with the bowed legs was our first star with the Broncos after the merger.

16. Peter Forsberg.
The guy from Sweden had more ability than any guy who laced up the skates. He could never stay healthy.

15. Andres Galarraga.
"The Big Cat." Popular. The homerun he hit in Florida against Kevin Brown traveled more than 500 feet. A cancer survivor.

14. Shannon Sharpe.
Late round pick who could only run two patterns when he came to Denver. Looks like a cinch Hall of Famer.

13. Carmelo Anthony.
Another prep. The best is ahead. He has the ability to do more than just score.

12. Matt Holliday.
Just a pup. Won the batting title and Scott Boras is going to make him very rich.

11. David Thompson.
Denver Nuggets. Remember the night he scored 73 points? He played in the Rafters. He had a great first step.

10. Dennis Smith.
Broncos Safety. Rugged and tough when he and Atwater played together. You didn't come into the middle if you were a receiver.

9. Larry Walker.
Colorado Rockies. Five-tool guy who won a batting title. He could hit, hit with power. Run, throw and catch the ball. The best instincts of any guy who ever played here.

8. Randy Gradishar.
The best linebacker ever coached and the best middle linebacker the Broncos ever had. He'd find you if you stayed in bounds and he didn't come out in passing situations.

7. Joe Sakic.
The captain of the Colorado Avalanche. Eighteen consecutive years with the same team. He's very much involved in the community.

6. Dan Issel.
"The House." The pride of Batavia, Illinois and the University of Kentucky had a great run here. Just a consistent player who gave you a go every night. Lost his teeth in Junior High in a phys ed class.

5. Terrell Davis.
The best 6th round pick ever. The MVP in the Super Bowl vs. Green Bay. He got stronger as the game went on. He developed the Bronco Salute. What a shame when he got hurt.

4. Alex English.
The Nuggets all time leading scorer. He didn't look strong, but he was and he was tough. What a great day February 1, 1980 was. Acquired Alex from Indiana in exchange for George McGinnis.

3. Todd Helton.
His numbers are right there with guys in the Hall. His critics complain he doesn't hit homeruns. He hit 49 before the humidor was introduced. He had the most important hit of the season, the ninth inning homerun against the Dodgers.

2. Patrick Roy.
Was in-goal two Stanley cups. He's in the NHL Hall of Fame. He even has a street named after him.

1. John Elway.
Was there ever a question? He owns the town. He wasn't a bad baseball player either. He played in the Yankee chain before the NFL.

We asked our audience: "Who are the 20 best-ever athletes who have competed for the Avs, Nuggets, Broncos or Rockies?" This is what they said:

20. Troy Tulowitzki and Matt Holliday.
If someone reads this book in 10 years, it would be pretty stupid not to have included these two rising stars.

19. Shannon Sharpe.
The Hall is waiting.

18. Gary Zimmerman.
As good a tackle as we've had. He played most of his time with the Vikings. In the Hall.

17. Karl Mecklenberg.
Never took a play off.

16. Andres Galarraga.
The Big Cat. Will anyone ever forget the 500-foot homerun against Kevin Brown?

15. Peter Forsberg.
Has there ever been a more exciting player to watch?

14. Louie Wright.
Next to Champ he's the best cover man the Broncos have had.

13. Champ Bailey.
The only reason he's not number two is his short time with the Broncos.

12. Dan Issel.
He's in the Hall of Fame. He was a nightmare for big centers with his quickness.

11. Tom Nalen.
In Mike Shanahan's words: "The best center I have ever seen."

10. Carmelo Anthony.
He hasn't played many years but the fans love his ability. If only he can keep himself out of trouble.

9. Larry Walker.
The only five-tool player the Rockies have ever had.

8. Randy Gradishar.
We keep asking the question: Why isn't he in the Hall of Fame?

7. David Thompson.
Skywalker with the quickest first step ever.

6. Patrick Roy.

He came here late in his career. He was the missing link for the Stanley Cup.

5. Alex English.

The Nuggets all-time leading scorer.

4. Todd Helton.

His numbers are worthy of the Hall of Fame.

3. Terrell Davis.

John Elway summed it up: "He's the best back I have ever handed off to."

2. Joe Sakic.

The classy leader of the Avs.

1. John Elway.

He's the unanimous favorite. Hall of Fame quarterback. His restaurant is pretty good, too.

Karl Mecklenburg was the 310th player chosen in the 1983 draft—humble beginnings for an outstanding 12-year professional career as a linebacker for the Broncos. Never took a play off.

4. He started 141 of the 180 games he played.

3. He finished his career with 1,145 tackles and 79.5 sacks.

In the 1985 season he had 13 sacks. Twice in his career he had four sacks in a game.

2. He played in six Pro Bowls.

1. He played in three Super Bowls with the Broncos.

We asked Karl to name the five best backs he competed against. These are his picks:

5. Ronny Harmon.

A quick back.

4. Barry Sanders.

The Original.

3. Curt Warner.

Barry Sanders before Barry.

2. Walter Payton.

Constant effort.

1. Kevin Mack.

Tough guy.

Toughest Guys Ever To Play Football in Colorado

What can we say? You just don't mess with these guys.

10. Dennis Smith.
Broncos safety. He would run right through you, never formed up, and just had killer shots. Can you believe he and Ronnie Lott were in the same defensive backfield at USC?

9. Steve Atwater.
Broncos safety. Can anyone forget the hit he laid on Christian Okoye?

8. Hardy Brown.
Broncos. Only played one year,1960, and he was over the hill. But talk to Tom Landry. Nobody hit like Hardy.

7. John Lynch.
Still an All-Pro when it comes to sticking people.

6. Rick Dennison.
Denver Broncos, now the coordinator. No one took on guards better.

5. Royal Shepherd.
Farlen's coach was a linebacker for CU in the early 50s. He took on all comers.

4. John Farler.
CU, played 1965-67, and nobody fooled with him at practice. He was mean.

3. Jim David.
Defensive back at Colorado A&M. He wore that birdcage and no one could punch his ticket. Vicious tackler.

2. Joe Rizzo.
Denver Broncos, out of US Merchant Marine Academy. Played six years. A member of the Orange Crush. Nobody fooled with him.

1. Tom Brookshier.
CU defensive back. Went on to play for the Eagles. Attacked wide receivers. He challenged them before they got into their routes.

Note: Louis Wright was a true Shutdown Corner for the Denver Broncos. He was drafted out of San Jose State in the first round in 1975, and played in Denver for 12 years. A five-time Pro Bowl selection, Wright was twice named Most Valuable Defensive Player by his teammates. He was fast. He ran track in college, and ran the 100-yard dash in 9.6 seconds. With the Broncos, he played 166 games with 163 starts. He intercepted 26 passes and made 11 fumble recoveries. He's one of the Broncos all-time finest gentlemen. He's now a teacher at Mrachek Middle School, and an assistant coach for Rangeview High School football. We asked Louie to name the toughest wideouts to cover.

4. Cliff Branch.
Speed, speed and more speed.

3. Lynn Swann.
Never got the credit he deserved.

2. Jerry Rice.
Saw him near the end. He could turn you everywhere and get loose. Great route runner.

1. John Jeffers.
No hesitation. With the Chargers. Not only did he catch everything, he would knock you down. Just a great blocker. He and Dan Fouts were a great combination.

The Broncos acquired Rod Smith as a college free agent in 1994. Since then, he has racked up an impressive list of receptions and records. Bonus accomplishment: Rod is the best pitchman ever for Blackjack Pizza. His famous tagline: "Stick with the home team." Catchy . . . like Number 80. Due to hip injury and surgery, the Broncos placed Smith on the reserve-retired list in February 2008. We'll miss him on the field. He's had a great career. A lot of fans remember he had 208 yards receiving in one game—versus Atlanta in 2004. He had a franchise-record 1,602 yards receiving in 2000, plus a franchise-record of 113 one-season receptions in 2001. Having back-to-back 100-catch seasons in 2000 and 2001 marked a rare feat—it has happened only six other times in the NFL. Here's a list of some amazing numbers that illustrate Rod's career.

Total yards from-scrimmage: 11,737.
Rod is one of only 25 NFL players to reach 10,000 career receiving yards.

Total combined yards: 12,488.
More than any other player in Broncos history.

Career receptions: 849.
Receiving yards: 11,389.
Touchdown catches: 68.
With a total of 71 touchdowns overall.

Pro Bowls played: Three.
Consecutive games catching at least one pass: 124.

We asked Rod to name the toughest cornerbacks he has ever faced. These are his picks:

5. Terrel Buckley, Sam Madison and Dale Carter.
These guys gave me trouble.

4. Champ Bailey.
He became a teammate but I went against him many times. Bailey has the greatest instincts. You throw the ball and he's on it. He doesn't just knock the ball down—he gets interceptions.

3. Deion Sanders.
The best when beat, using great catch-up speed.

2. Charles Woodson.
He has all the skills.

1. James Hasty.
By far, the most physical. He started bumping when he got off the bus.

Note: Brett Clark, Colorado Avalanche defenseman, doesn't come off the ice much. In the 2006-07 season, he led the club in ice time, averaging 24 minutes a game. Brett finished second in scoring among defensemen, with a career-high 39 points. Brett is a big fan favorite. We asked him to list the top five toughest players in the NHL in his opinion.

5. Teemu Selanne.

Anaheim. Quick, gets in the shooting lanes.

4. Ryan Smyth.

Glad we have him.

3. Joe Thornton.

San Jose. Very fast, very strong.

2. Sidney Crosby.

Pittsburgh. The most skilled.

1. Jarome Iginla.

Calgary. Strong, big and nasty.

Five Toughest Centers :: Bill Hanzlik

Note: Bill Hanzlik was an All-American at Notre Dame and played basketball for the U.S. Olympic Team. He played in the NBA for 10 years, with the Sonics and the Nuggets. He has been around Denver since 1982. For the infamous 1997-98 season, Bill replaced Dick Motta as the Nuggets head coach. Let's all try to forget that season. Nowadays, Bill does the Nuggets post-game show on Altitude. When he played for Doug Moe, Doug would change up and have the 6-foot-7 Hanzlik guard big centers to drive them nuts. Bill names the toughest centers to defeat:

5. Kareem Abdul Jabbar.
The unstoppable shot.

4. Artis Gilmore.
Don't get him mad.

3. Hakeem Olajuwan.
Couldn't out-quick him.

2. David Robinson.
So long and fast.

1.Patrick Ewing.
He set the meanest screens.

Homegrown Basketball Pros

Thirteen men's basketball players from Colorado schools have played professional basketball in Denver. In chronological order:

13. Rodney White (2002.)
George Washington High School. The Nuggets got him from Detroit in a trade. George Washington was one of five high schools he attended before playing at Charlotte.

12. Chauncey Billups (1998-90.)
George Washington High School and University of Colorado. The All-American from CU was never used right. He averaged about 12 points per game. Now with the Pistons, he's one of the best.

11. Brooks Thompson (1996-97.)
Littleton High School. Only a cup of coffee with the Nuggets.

10. Mark Randall (1993-95.)
Cherry Creek High School. Limited action here. H's now a Nugget Ambassador and the kids love him.

9. Mike Higgins (1989-90.)
University of Northern Colorado. He was from Greeley. He's considered one of the best to come out of that city along with Larry Hofner and Theis Holland. Limited action with the Nuggets.

8. Joe Barry Carroll (1989-90.)
Denver East High School. The number one pick when he came out of Purdue. He played sparingly. In the one year, he averaged 11.9 points per game.

7. Eddie Hughes (1988-90.)
Colorado State University. Cat quick. Could distribute.

6. Glen Gondrezick (1979-83.)
Boulder High School. By far the most popular on this list, he was a hell-for-leather kind of guy.

5. Dave Bustion (1972-73.)
University of Denver. Just one year here. Played sparingly. In 47 games he averaged three points a game.

4. Chuck Williams (1971-72; 75-77.)
University of Colorado. Two tours here. He was a solid, dependable player.

3. Byron Beck (1967-77.)
University of Denver. Ten years here and he has his number retired, which is curious. He averaged 11 points per game.

2. Chuck Gardner (1967-68.)

University of Colorado. Played with the Denver Rockets sparingly. Went back to coach at CU with Sox Walseth.

1. Lonnie Wright (1967-71.)

Colorado State University. He was also a Denver Broncos defensive back. In 14 years he averaged 12 points per game. He could cover.

Five Favorite Interviewees :: Woody Paige

Note: Our good friend Woody Paige has been a sports columnist for more than 35 years. He writes for *The Denver Post*. In 2004, he moved to New York to be one of the hosts of ESPN's *Cold Pizza*. We're glad he's back in Denver now, but you can still see him on ESPN as a panelist on *Around the Horn*. Everyone knows that the Wood Man's roots are in Tennessee. What you probably don't know—or don't remember—is that Woody did a talk show in the early 80s on KWBZ and KLAK with Irv and Joe. Woody has a talent for interviewing sports stars and fun-loving people. We asked him to name his five favorite interviewees.

5. Glen Gondrezek.
One of the most popular Nuggets. A strong sixth man, he was in Denver for four years. He grew up in Boulder. Glen had the talent to play pro baseball, but he chose basketball. A real character. Great sense of humor. One time, returning home from a trip, he made an entrance by coming down the baggage chute. He has been a UNLV men's basketball analyst on the radio for the past 15 years.

4. Mike Ricci.
Played for the Philadelphia Flyers, Quebec Nordiques, Colorado Avs, San Jose Sharks and Phoenix Coyotes. He had the best long hair, and no teeth. Loose as a goose. Fun to interview.

3. Dante Bichette.
"Alphonse" hit a three-run homer in the 14th inning of the first game at Coors Field. The Rockies won 11-9 over the New York Mets. Bichette was wild, loose from another planet.

2. Doug Moe.
He had been an ABA all-star. Coached San Antonio, the Denver Nuggets and Philadelphia. A lighthearted guy. Never took himself too seriously. Affectionately called his wife "Big Jane," or "Big" for short.

1. Tom Jackson.
He was a solid weak-side linebacker for the Denver Broncos, and part of the famous Orange Crush. He always gave a great quote, and he loved to dig John Madden.

Dan's Best Sportswriters

Dan Creedon has a great eye for talent. He's the former sports editor of Boulder's *Daily Camera*. He retired in 2001 after 39 years. Dan's Favorite Moment in Sports: 1956, Memorial Day, Mickey Mantle hits the façade at Yankee Stadium. We had a conversation with Dan about the best sportswriters he ever hired. Here are the names he listed.

4. Michael Knisley.

A Jack Nicklaus look-alike. He was a student at CU when Dan found him. Dan liked the way he wrote a story. Knisley had a solid run with the *Sporting News*. He's a senior editor at ESPN.com.

3. Ed Werder.

Dan recognized how goal-oriented Ed was, how he would dig for a story. In 1982, he graduated from UNC in Greeley with a journalism degree. Dan found him in Tucson. From 1984 to 1989, he covered the Broncos for the *Camera*. Ed is now a regular with ESPN, reporting on the NFL. Before ESPN, he was a NFL correspondent for CNN. Also, he covered the Dallas Cowboys for the *Dallas Morning News* and the *Fort Worth Star Telegram*.

2. Doug Looney.

He's a graduate of CU's school of journalism and is now on the school's advisory board. His father, Robert C. Looney, worked at the *Daily Camera* for 42 years and was managing editor from 1964 to 1970. Dan loved how irreverent Doug was, and his sense of humor. Later, Doug had a great run with *Sports Illustrated* and the *Christian Science Monitor*.

1. Rick Reilly.

Rick is a Boulder native. Dan hired Rick when he was a student at CU. Dan recognized his talent, his sense of humor, his ability to tell stories—Rick could make everything a fun story to read. Reilly worked for the *Camera* from 1979 to 1981. He moved on to *The Denver Post*, the *Los Angeles Times* and *Sports Illustrated*, writing the back page column called "The Life of Reilly." He recently moved to ESPN. Rick has won the national Sportswriter of the Year award 11 times. He's a prolific writer: his books include a novel entitled, *Missing Links*, and it's sequel, *Shanks for Nothing*. He co-wrote the screenplay for *Leatherheads*, a screwball comedy set during the early days of football, directed by and starring George Clooney.

Best Three-Point Shooters

Denver Nuggets fans have been screaming for a three-point shooter in this decade. Here are the best long-range guys ever to play for the Nuggets.

10. Allen Iverson.
He does most of his work at the free-throw line and driving, but he can nail the three.

9. Nick Van Exel.
He got into it with the fans but the lefty could shoot. In 1999 he had 133 threes.

8. Voshon Lenard.
In 2000 he had 382 threes. Injuries slowed him down.

7. Ralph Simpson.
The big guard out of Michigan State had a soft touch from the top of the key.

6. Dale Ellis.
The Nuggets got him late and coach Dan Issel said he's got something left in the tank. For three years, 1995-1997, he led the team in three pointers with 448 threes.

5. John Roche.
John was deadly from the outside. He is one of three players in NBA history to hit seven three-pointers in a single quarter.

4. Mike Evans.
The best, not only here but in the league. Dribbling to his left, squaring up, then getting great spring on his jump shot.

3. Chris Jackson/Mahmoud Abdul-Rauf.
Should have been the best ever because his rotation was the best. He got involved with the anthem and was never the same. He refused to stand for the national anthem before games because he felt that the flag was a symbol of oppression.

2. Kiki Vandeweghe.
The best ever here, inside and outside. You had to respect his ability to drive. He made his opponent back off. He could always get a shot off by looking at your feet and then hoisting up a quick shot.

1. Michael Adams.
The little gunner from Boston College had 630 threes in his career as a Nugget. Closest to him is 182 away. He had the fans on their feet every time he got the ball.

Broncos Trivia Tutorial #2

Here's another list of stuff that every Broncos fan is required to know but otherwise serves no significant purpose. Listed in order of how important or obvious each item is in the larger universe of Broncos knowledge.

15. Who's The Greatest?
Orange Crush defensive end Lyle Alzado boxed Muhammad Ali in an 8-round exhibition in 1979.

14. Humble beginnings.
Back in the day, Patriots superstar head coach Bill Belichick was assistant special teams coach and gofer for Red Miller's Broncos.

13. Barrel Man!
Tim McKernan, also known as Barrel Man, attended all Broncos home games wearing nothing but a barrel for 30 years. Brr. In 2003, for medical reasons, he started wearing the barrel for only part of each game, weather permitting. He retired in 2007.

12. Covered.
The first Bronco ever to appear on the cover of *Sports Illustrated* was a member of the Orange Crush, Rubin Carter, in October 1977.

11 Ironman.
You could say that Pat Bowlen, the owner of the Denver Broncos, maintains an "active lifestyle." He has competed in the Ironman Triathlon, a grueling test of endurance that involves a 2.4-miles swim, 112-mile bicycle race and a 26.2-miles run. Go Pat!

10. Jerry's last game.
Jerry Rice wore a Broncos uniform in his final pro game. He played briefly with Denver for the 2005 preseason before he retired.

9. Name is Bucky Bronco.
The large fiberglass Bronco statue on the south scoreboard at Invesco Field, was introduced at Mile High Stadium in 1975. Bucky is 27 feet tall.

8. Bad trades.
Willie Brown signed with the Broncos in 1963 and was exceptional at grabbing interceptions. Coach Lou Saban came in and traded Brown to the Oakland Raiders after the 1966 season, where he made trouble for the Broncos for the next 12 years. Brown was inducted into the Hall of Fame in 1984. Bonus: Saban traded rookie Carley Culp to the Chiefs. He became one of the NFL's best nose guards.

7. Receiver and punter.
Billy Van Heusen was one of the Broncos best receivers, with 82 receptions for 1,684 yards from 1968 to 1976. He also punted 574 times, averaging more than 41 yards per punt. He and his son are now in the sports nutrition business in Denver.

6. Tom Rouen.

He punted 641 times during his career with the Broncos from 1993 to 2002. Rouen grew up in Littleton.

5. KHOW.

Bronco John Lynch's father played linebacker for the Pittsburgh Steelers. Later, Irv Brown and Joe Williams worked for Lynch senior for a while at radio station KHOW.

4. Record kicks.

Broncos Gene Mingo and Rich Karlis had each kicked five field goals in a single game. It was two different games, of course; Gene kicked in one, Rich kicked in the other. In 1997, Jason Elam broke their record with six field goals in a single game, against the Chiefs.

3. Ice Bowl connection.

Long before he became Denver's head coach, Dan Reeves threw a touchdown pass for the Dallas Cowboys in the 1967 game against the Packers that ultimately sent Green Bay to the very first Super Bowl.

2. The swimming Elway.

Janet Elway left a legacy at Stanford as a world-class swimmer. Janet had her sights set on the 1980 Olympics in Moscow but the U.S. boycotted. Her children are outstanding athletes, too. Plus, she founded Janet's Camp, a charity to benefit economically disadvantaged kids through the YMCA summer camps.

1. Stanford Band connection.

John Elway was Stanford's quarterback in one of the most memorable college football games of all time. The Stanford band prematurely celebrated "victory" by swarming the field while the Cal team orchestrated a rugby-style kick-off return, throwing five lateral passes to reach the end zone and win the game in the final seconds.

Five Tough Offensive Linemen :: Alfred Williams

Note: Alfred Williams was an All-American linebacker at CU in 1990. He was the 1990 Butkus Award Winner. In his college career, he had 263 tackles and 35 sacks. The Bengals drafted him in the first round in 1991. He came to the Broncos in 1996. That year, he was named All-Pro defensive end. He was part of Denver's Super Bowl glory in 1997 and 1998. Alfred retired from pro football after the 1999 season, but you can hear him on FM 104.3 The Fan, afternoons from 1 to 3. We asked Alfred to name the toughest five offensive linemen he competed against.

5. Anthony Munoz.
Strongest hands. Great balance.

4. Richmond Webb.
Long arms. Great balance.

3. Tony Jones.
Big. Strong. Smart.

2. Willie Roaf.
The meanest. Quick, big and strong.

1. Jonathan Ogden.
Long arms. With a nasty disposition.

Note: David Treadwell was a soccer player who ended up as a solid place-kicker. He was a walk-on for the Clemson Tigers in 1984. From 1984 to 1987, he connected on 47 out of 66 field goals and was 92/93 on extra points. Clemson fans love him because his kicks helped the Tigers beat Georgia in two consecutive seasons.

David kicked for the Broncos from 1989 to 1992, and was chosen for the Pro Bowl in his rookie season. During his years with the Broncos, he had a field goal percentage of 77.9 percent, making 99 of 127 attempts. He played for the NY Giants 1993-94. After his pro football career, David was the first sports anchor on Fox 31 working with Ron Zappolo and Libby Weaver. He's now a developer in the Metro Area. Bonus factoid: He has a degree in Electrical Engineering. We asked Dave to list his top five most memorable kicks.

5. 1986.
Between the Hedges. Clemson at Georgia. Clemson wins 31-28. I hit a 46-yarder as time expires.

4. 1987.
28-yard field goal beats Georgia again 23-21 with 2 seconds left on the clock.

3. 1990.
At Kansas City. A 22-yarder as time expires. Broncos win 24-23.

2. 1992.
At Houston. Monday Night Football. Walk-off 37-yarder to win it.

1. 1992.
Broncos vs. Houston in the Divisional Playoff game. Hit a 28-yarder to win it.

From Player to Coach

Are you a better pro coach if you were once a pro player? Not necessarily. The most successful coach in Denver is Mike Shanahan. He didn't get to play much football because he lost a kidney. Sometimes a playing career works against you as a coach. Witness Ted Williams with the Washington Senators. That didn't work. But it sure gains respect from your players when you've been in their shoes and played well. Here are the ten best former pro players who coached a Denver pro team.

10. Bill Hanzlik.

He coached the Nuggets only one year and never really had a chance to succeed. He won only 11 games. They had a bad roster. One guy who could play was LaPhonso Ellis. Hanzlik was an All-American at Notre Dame and played on the U.S. Olympic team. He was a real gamer here, did all the dirty work. Solid defender. Never took a play off.

9. Larry Brown.

He was the fourth-winningest coach in NBA history. He coached the Nuggets for four years. In 1974-75 the club was 65-19. Larry starred at North Carolina and was a three time ABA All-Star. He won a gold medal playing on our 1964 Olympic team. He coached the Olympic team in 2004. He is the only man to have played and coached basketball in the Olympics.

8. Lou Saban.

He coached the Denver Broncos for two years, 1967-1969. At the time he was the highest paid coach in the AFL with $50,000 a year. He was average here but had great success with the Buffalo Bills with OJ Simpson and the Electric Company. He was a heck of a player. He played at Indiana—all Big Ten as a quarterback, and all Big Ten as a fullback the following year. Then he played for the Cleveland Browns. In the All-American Conference, he was a linebacker who was voted to the All-Star team twice. His cousin is Nick Saban, coach of the Alabama Crimson Tide.

7. Alex Hanum.

He coached the Denver Rockets for three years. Just a so-so record here but next to Phil Jackson, he's the only guy to coach two different teams to an NBA title, St. Louis and Philadelphia. He also won an ABA title in Oakland. Alex also coached Wilt Chamberlain. He was a great player at Hamilton High School in LA, then USC before going pro with Oshkosh. He was inducted into the Basketball Hall of Fame in 1998. He passed away in 2002.

6. Joel Quenneville.

Colorado Avalanche coach. He played 13 seasons in the NHL. A tough defenseman. He played with five different teams. He even played in Denver for two-and-a-half years. He never backed down—he had 705 penalty minutes in 803 games.

5. Buddy Bell.

The Rockies' third manager. A solid Big Leaguer. Buddy was a career .280 hitter with Cleveland, Texas and Cincinnati. Mr. Consistency with the bat, and he could play third.

4. Don Baylor.

"Groove." The Rockies' first manager during the early touch years. He was a great player, 19 years in the Bigs, five different teams. A career .260 hitter who belted 338 homeruns. He would take one for the team and got hit a lot. A terrific tight end in high school. The University of Texas wanted him.

3. Doug Moe.

"The Big Stuff." Yes, he's the winningest coach in Nuggets history with 432 wins. Yes, he coached San Antonio and Philadelphia. But people forget how good a player he was. Two-time All-American at North Carolina, five years as an ABA All-Star. Al Bianchi, a great scout, says Moe was the toughest guy to lace up the sneakers.

2. Dan Reeves.

He was an all-purpose back with Dallas. He was a quarterback at South Carolina. Very versatile. When he played for Tom Landry, it was like having a coach on the field. Dan's coaching record with Denver is 117-79, and the Broncos went to three Super Bowls.

1. Dan Issel.

He's in the Basketball Hall of Fame. An All-American at Kentucky, he's in the Nuggets record book in nine categories. He scored 16,589 points. He coached the Nuggets for three years 1992-95, then 1999-2002. A record of 159-148.

Bonus:

Mac Speedie coached the Broncos for two years. He played for the Cleveland Browns. Otto Graham said he was the equal to Dante Lavelli.

Great Colorado Golfers

Colorado has an embarrassment of riches when it comes to golf. Our state is home to some of the most beautiful courses we've ever played—and many good municipal courses, too. Colorado also has thousands of outstanding golfers. It was tough to name· just a handful who have enriched Colorado's golf reputation.

Jill McGill.

One of the most popular women in golf, Jill was born and raised in Denver, skiing in winter and playing golf in summer. She accepted a golf scholarship at the University of Southern California, where she was a two-time All-American. She won the U. S. Women's Amateur title in 1993. She's on the LPGA tour and is an avid surfer, now living in San Diego.

Warren F. Smith, Jr.

He was a popular head pro at Cherry Hills CC from 1963 to 1990. He still lives in Denver. He hit seven birdies in a row during the 1955 Texas open, and played in three PGA championships. He's in the Colorado Golf Hall of Fame.

Joan Birkland.

She's known for tennis, but wasn't too shabby at golf, winning several CWGA titles in the 1960s. She was named outstanding amateur athlete in the state in 1962. She's now the executive director of Sportswomen of Colorado, an organization that honors and supports girl and women athletes.

Pat Lange.

LPGA Master Professional and teaching pro. Having been an instructor for many years, she saw that women could play better golf if they had proper equipment. In 1992 she founded Lange Golf, specializing custom-fitted golf clubs specifically made for women. The company is based in Georgetown.

David Duval.

He lives in Denver. A four-time All-American at Georgia Tech. Earned his PGA tour card in 1995. He won 13 PGA Tour tournaments from 1997 to 2001. Tied for second in the Masters in 1998 and 2001. He shot 59 in the final round of the Bob Hope Classic in 1999.

Dow Finsterwald.

Had 12 wins on the PGA Tour in his career. Won the 1958 PGA Championship. Finished in the money in 72 consecutive tournaments. Had the lowest scoring average of any pro in 1957. For 28 years, he was the popular golf director at The Broadmoor in Colorado Springs.

Hale Irwin.

One of the world's best golfers. Won three U.S. Open titles. At CU, he played great football. He was also the 1967 NCAA Golf Champion. Between 1971 and 1994, he had 19 wins on the PGA Tour. Since 1995, he has won 45 Champions Tour titles. He's also a golf course architect—he designed Indian Peaks Golf Course in Lafayette, among others.

We have so many good young golfers in our state. I work with First Tee of Denver, an organization that promotes golf as a tool to educate kids academically, socially and physically. It gives inner-city and disadvantaged kids a chance to practice and play. I like it because it teaches core values. Here are some of our future golf stars and what they've done in the Colorado Junior Golf Association. There's an alphabet full of talented kids, but I stopped at the letter "D." You get the picture.

Jack Adolfson.
Age 12. Longmont. Finished in the top five at six CJGA events and tied for second at the Junior World Qualifier.

Nicholas Allen.
Age 15. Littleton. Plays out of Raccoon Creek GC. He placed in the top 10 at the CHSAA 5A State Championship.

Branden Barron.
Age 17. Plays out of South Suburban Family Sports Center. He had victories at the Aurora City Junior Championship, a CJGA event at Walking Stick. Went to California as a member of the Junior America's Cup team.

Zahkai Brown.
Age 18. Arvada. Plays out of Indian Tree GC. He won the CHSAA 5A State Championship and a PGA Junior Series Event.

Bethany Buchner.
Age 16. Loveland. Plays out of Ptarmigan Country Club. She qualified for the USGA Girls Junior Amateur, won the Callaway Junior World Qualifier and was the runner-up at the CHSAA 5A State Championship.

Wyndham Clark.
Age 13. Greenwood Village. Took top honors at the City of Aurora Junior Championship. Was the youngest player to advance to match play at the CGA Junior Match Play Championship.

Brooke Collins.
Age 18. Louisville. Plays at Omni Interlocken GC. Placed first in the CHSAA 5A State Championship and second in both the CWGA Junior Stroke Play Championship and the CJGA Tournament of Champions.

Claudia Davis.
Age 12. Centennial. Participated in eight CJGA Junior Series Events where she placed in the top 10 every time. Took top honors at the 11-12 Junior World Qualifier and the City of Aurora Junior Championship.

Calvin Dorsey.

Age 12. Denver. Plays out of Meridian GC. Placed in the top five at six events including a win at Evergreen GC.

Katy Dyachkova.

Age 13. Centennial. Practices at South Suburban GC. She won three CJGA events and placed second at the City of Aurora Junior Championship.

Note: John Edwards did graduate study in communication research at the University of Colorado. He has a great golf newspaper called *Colorado Golfer*. He was kind enough to share his paper's 2007 picks for best golf courses in Colorado, based on votes from pros. He and his staff don't vote; they tabulate ballots and interpret the results.

Toughest Public Course

2. Murphy Creek Golf Course, Aurora.
1. Riverdale Dunes Golf Course, Brighton.

Best Value for Public Daily Fee (Green fee under $50)

2. Meadow Hills Golf Course, Aurora.
1. Riverdale Dunes Golf Course, Brighton.

Riverdale Dunes, a links-style course, once again received more total votes and more first place votes than any other course. It has won the award in every poll since 1998 followed by Lakewood's Fox Hollow Golf Course. The Dunes course was also selected again as the toughest of the public courses, followed by Murphy Creek that will be hosting the U.S. Mid-Amateur Tournament in 2008.

Best Premium Public Course (Green fee over $50)

Note: The premier public courses that charge more than $50 a day for golf and mandatory cart are grouped together. Designed by famous architects these "country clubs for a day" cost considerably more to build, and cater to corporate outings and affluent golfers. Consequently we follow the *Golf Digest* magazine classification system to define these courses.

5. Omni Interlocken Golf Club, Broomfield.
4. Highlands Ranch Golf Club, Highlands Ranch.
3. Vista Ridge Golf Club, Erie.
2. Bear Dance Golf Club, Larkspur.

The Golf Club at Bear Dance, the Home of the Colorado PGA, once again placed second in the voting and was again ranked the toughest of the premier courses.

1. The Ridge at Castle Pines North, Castle Rock.

The Ridge at Castle Pines North once again led the voting earning the most first place and total votes. Located along the cliffs between the Country Club at Castle Pines and Sanctuary, the course was designed by Tom Weiskopf.

Toughest Premium Public Course

2. The Ridge at Castle Pines North, Castle Rock.
1. Bear Dance Golf Club, Larkspur.

Best Value for Premium Public Course

2. Vista Ridge Golf Club, Erie.
1. Bear Dance Golf Club, Larkspur.
Best Mountain Course
5. Haymaker Golf Course, Steamboat Springs.
4. Keystone River Course, Keystone.
3. Pole Creek Golf Course, Winter Park.
2. The Raven at Three Peaks, Silverthorne.
1. Breckenridge Golf Club, Breckenridge.

Breckenridge once again dominated the mountain courses that are open to the public. It had the most first-place votes and twice the votes of second place Raven at Three Peaks. The selection of Breckenridge as the toughest mountain course surprises many public golfers. They don't ever play from the way-back Nicklaus tees that stretch the course to 7,229 yards. The professionals play from the back and have to make the long drives over wetlands and beaver ponds.

Toughest Mountain Course

2. The Raven at Three Peaks, Silverthorne.
1. Breckenridge Golf Club, Breckenridge.

Best Value for a Mountain Course

2. Pole Creek Golf Course, Winter Park.
1. Haymaker Golf Course, Steamboat Springs.

Best Resort Course

Note: The resort category requires that players must be staying at the resort or be a member to play the course. Some courses at mountain resorts do not fall into this category since they allow same day public play at slower times of the year.

5. The Broadmoor, West Course, Colorado Springs.
4. Club at Cordillera, Valley Course.
3. Red Sky, Fazio Course, Wolcott.
2. Red Sky, Norman Course, Wolcott.
1. The Broadmoor, East Course, Colorado Springs.

Toughest Resort Course

2. Red Sky, Norman Course.
Most professionals have now played both of the Red Sky courses but tended to lump them together.

1.The Broadmoor, East Course.
The Broadmoor East Course dominated the Best and Toughest categories. The course and the famous hotel garnered most of the first place votes and twice the total votes of the runner-up. First designed in 1918 by Donald Ross, the traditional favorite is still considered the toughest test of resort golf in Colorado.

Best Value for a Resort Course

2. The Broadmoor, East Course.
While the golf rates at The Broadmoor are not as high as some mountain resorts, the room rates to get access to the course are considerably higher.

1. Inverness Golf Club, Englewood.
Once the site of the Colorado Open, Inverness is very familiar to PGA professionals. It offers reasonably priced weekend golf and lodging escape packages to golfers that stay just to be able to play the course.

Best Private Course

5. Denver Country Club, Denver.
4. Country Club of the Rockies, Edwards.
3. Columbine Country Club, Littleton.
2. Castle Pines Golf Club, Castle Rock.
1. Cherry Hills Country Club, Englewood.
The traditional design and the excellent conditioning earned Cherry Hills more votes, more first place voters and more total points to surpass the Jack Nicklaus-designed Castle Pines Golf Club. These two courses dominate the voting.

Toughest Private Course

3. Bear Creek Golf Club, Denver.

2. Cherry Hills Country Club, Englewood.

1. Castle Pines Golf Club, Castle Rock.

The Colorado professionals, PGA Tour players and even the general public recognize the difficulty of the course. At 7,599 yards with a slope rating of 150, Castle Pines may not be the longest but it is certainly the toughest in the state.

Best Nine Hole Course

2. Lincoln Park Golf Course, Grand Junction.

1. City Park Nine Golf Course, Fort Collins.

The Fort Collins City Park Golf Course and Grand Junction's pioneer Lincoln Park Golf Course are always the leaders. The mature courses are in large municipal parks located in the center of their towns. Only about half the professionals cast votes on the nine-hole courses. They don't play pro-ams at nine-hole courses so they are not as familiar with these courses.

Colorado golfers can play warm desert-style golf during the winter without driving past Pueblo. I love to make the drive south—it's only about 2 hours from Denver. The weather patterns are warmer and there's more sunshine in Pueblo than in other parts of Colorado. Walking Stick Golf Course is my favorite. It hosted the U.S. Women's Public Links Championship in 2006. Desert Hawk at Pueblo West is another good one. Below are my picks vis-à-vis John Edwards' picks.

Toughest Public Course:
Legacy Ridge. The rough kills me. If I make bogie on the par 5 on the front nine, I'm thrilled.

Best Premium Public Course:
I like the Omni. It's a beautiful course, a tough course. Make mine the Omni.

Toughest Premium Public Course:
Bear Dance took me to my knees.

Best Value Premium Golf Course:
I like Vista Ridge. Tough layout.

Best Mountain Course:
Glenwood Springs is the toughest by far. It's tight and everything runs off the mountain.

Toughest Course:
Glenwood Springs.

Best Value Course:
Glenwood Springs.

Best Resort Course:
The Broadmoor. It is special. I love the course.

Best Value:
I like The Broadmoor.

Best Private Course:
Make mine Castle Pines. Shout out to Jack Vickers and Larry Thiel: Let the media have a day. Touch course except for Number 17.

Toughest Private Course:
Castle Pines.

Best Nine Hole Course:
City Park. It has tradition.

Best Public Golf Courses

We asked our listeners to name the best public golf courses in the metro area and beyond. Here are their responses.

20. **Springhill in Aurora.**
19. **Links at Highlands Ranch.**
18. **Applewood.**
17. **Overland.**
16. **Meadow Hills.**
15. **Green Valley Ranch.**
14. **South Suburban.**
13. **Park Hill.**
12. **Bear Dance.**
11. **Eagle Trace.**
10. **Broadlands in Broomfield.**
9. **Arrowhead.**
8. **Indian Tree.**
7. **Fox Hollow.**
6. **Denver's City Park.**
5. **Legacy Ridge.**
4. **Heritage at Westmoor.**
3. **Ridge at Castle Pines North.**
2. **Fossil Trace.**
1. **Riverdale Dunes.**

What We'll Miss About The International

In 2007, the PGA Tour tournament known as The International at Castle Pines ended its 21-year run. They couldn't find a sponsor. Tiger opted out. It was over. Here's a look back at some things we'll miss about The (now-defunct) International.

4. Big names in golf coming to town.
Past winners included Greg Norman, Davis Love III, Phil Mickelson, Vijay Singh and Ernie Els. Plus, 197 international players from 38 countries played in the event over the years.

3. $10 Million.
That's the amount donated by the event over the years to the Boys & Girls Club of Metro Denver. Jack Vickers did a lot of good for charity with this tournament.

2. Modified Stableford Scoring.
A per-hole scoring system designed to reward risk taking. A higher score is preferable to a lower score. We're confused already. This system made The International fairly unique.

1. Milkshakes.
Served in the locker room.

Note: Boxer Dave Sidwell takes us back to the days of the Denver Rocks, a now-defunct boxing club sponsored by Bill Daniels, the father of cable TV. Dave was part of a stable of Denver fighters trained by Bobby Lewis in the 1970s and 80s. In 1968, Lewis coached former world heavyweight champion George Foreman to an Olympic gold medal. He also coached the United States Olympic boxing team in 1972. He made a mark on Denver boxing. Remember, when these guys were fighting, there was only one champion, and only eight divisions in boxing. There were no "alphabet soup" titles. Dave lists the top Denver boxers trained by Bobby.

8. Lonnie Smith, Lightweight.

Lonnie was the only fighter in our stable who won the title outright. He beat a then-undefeated Billy Costello in 1979 but only held the belt for 8 months—losing it to Rene Arandardo. Lonnie's victory over Costello was a huge upset because at the time Costello had successfully defended his title 7 times and won all of those defenses by knock out. Lonnie was by far and away the best pure boxer of our bunch. He had great hand speed as well as great feet and could throw punches from all angles. He was also almost impossible to hit when he was at his best. The common thought at the time was that he couldn't punch but when he fought Costello he was 21-0 and 13 of his victories were won by knockouts. He really was very strong and could "bust you up" with his left hook. Lonnie's biggest problem was a common thread in the boxing world: he had an idiot relative managing his career after he won the title. He signed a contract for the Costello fight and the contract had incentives attached that would pay him $300K if he knocked out Costello. That was a huge payday for a lightweight fight back in the late 70s. It was so big he never got his money. His lawyer screwed Lonnie. Lonnie's lawyer and manager spent money from the fight they did not have and they also scheduled his first title defense against a 6-foot "banger" by the name of Rene Arandardo. They also accepted the fight at the Olympic Auditorium in L.A. where Arandardo grew up. Arandardo's record at the time of making the fight with Lonnie was 28-0. All the fights were knockout wins. To make matters worse Bobby had a heart attack two months prior to the fight. Leroy Jones and I conducted his training regimen. Lonnie trained hard, as always, but lack of money and mismanagement of his resources were big distractions. On the night of the fight, the Olympic was electric—and all the excitement was generated by Arandardo. The Olympic holds almost 10,000 for boxing and it seemed like every seat was occupied by one of Arandardo's cousins. Lonnie was uninspired at best and lost by a knockout in the second round. He never got another shot but still continues to fight. He lives in Denver and is trying to establish a gym on his own in Park Hill. His health is good and he continues to be a good guy.

7. Larry Barnes, Welterweight.

Larry's tenure with our stable was brief but he could have been a great fighter. Larry was a wrestler from Lincoln High School in Denver. He walked into our gym at Bobby's request after he saw Larry win the Class B welterweights title in the Golden Glove tournament. Prior to coming to our gym at the Albany Hotel, all of us trained at the Punch Bowl in the Elks building on 14th Street downtown. I knew Larry a little from there and I also knew that he was in the process of going to wrestle at CU just before they disbanded the program. Larry only had the same number of fights as me: seven. Larry fought right handed and had good athletic skills. He was a great puncher and was a polished, skillful fighter far beyond his experience. Unfortunately Larry had a medical problem with his eyes that prevented him from fighting after those seven bouts. He won all of those fights, six by knockout. He and the others in the gym, particularly Larry Bonds had wars when they sparred. Larry is living in Denver and is an electrician.

6. Billy Parks, Welterweight.

Bill had an uncanny resemblance to Ali. He was tall for a welterweight (6-foot-0) and was blessed with great speed in his hands, body movement and his feet. Billy was also adept at impersonating fighters, particularly Ali. His style was almost identical to the way Ali punched and moved. Ron Lyle always insisted that Billy be his sparring partner prior to fighting Ali. It was a huge advantage for Ron in his fight with Ali. Billy could also emulate almost any fighter of that era and do it perfectly. He was a very accomplished welterweight himself. He finished his career with a record of 36-4-1 and went the distance with Wilfredo Benetez and many other great fighters of his era. He still lives in Denver and just retired after working for Greyhound for the last 20 years.

5. Larry Bonds, Welterweight.

Larry Bonds was a left-handed fighter with immense talent and skills. With the exception of me and probably Lyle, all of the fighters in this stable had great speed both upstairs and down. Larry was left handed and a bit unorthodox in body lean and punching position. He could throw a fairly stiff punch leaning backward or be completely hunched forward and punch. He was similar to Lonnie in that he was very hard to hit. Unlike Lonnie, who used his feet to avoid punches, Larry used his great ability to lean, slide and slip out of harm's way and always be in position to hit you back. This ability made him a great counter puncher and his hard speed enabled him to be first as well. He could hit an opponent six times in two seconds. The results made him a top ranked welterweight and led to a championship fight against Sugar Ray Leonard in the Carrier Dome in Syracuse. Larry got TKO-ed in the eleventh round in the scheduled fifteen-round fight in 1980. I was in his corner. At no time was he overwhelmed by the circumstances of the moment. Sugar Ray was winning the fight but not by much. Larry just could not hurt Sugar at all and eventually took too many punches. Larry only fought two more times after this fight and very sadly drifted into some trouble. Larry always worked another job while he was fighting. We all did except Ronnie because he was under contract with Bill Daniels and was okay, momentarily speaking. The last I heard, Larry was living in Chicago.

4. Eric Sedillo, Light Heavyweight.

Although Eric was not "one of us" because he was not directly trained under Bobby Lewis, he was at our gym training probably two or three nights a week. He was a great guy and walked around at 195 lbs. When he fought, there was no cruiser weight division so he had to cut a lot of weight to compete at 175 lbs. Eric was a rock. He was a bull to spar and none of us liked to spar him, including Lyle, because he only knew one speed. He hit like a horse and had a good chin so he was a guy most of us tried to avoid sparring. When Lyle and Eric worked out together we all stopped and watched. Eric, like all of us, could not take too many shots from Ronnie but he stayed right with him for the most part. Ron would always use 20 ounce when he sparred with Eric but that really didn't make much difference. Eric's record was 18-2 and he fought a fellow by the name of Bob Foster who KO-ed him. That was no disgrace. He always had a bad back and this condition forced him out of boxing but this guy was a quality fighter with a huge heart. He lives in Denver and owns a concrete business.

3. Dave Sidwell, Heavyweight.

It might be hard to be objective about myself but I'll try. I got into boxing pretty late. My football career at CU consisted of getting hurt, getting operated on, and rehabbing my injuries just in time for the fall to roll around and get hurt again. I had four major surgeries during my time at CU so I did the logical thing: I started boxing. There was very little heavyweight competition in the Golden Gloves. I won the open class HWT title in 1967-68-69. I also won the 6 state regional tournaments those years. But because of spring football practice, I was never able to go to the national tournament. That was probably good! My amateur career consisted of 33 fights over about five years. I won them all. Then Ron Lyle was released from prison and ended my reign as the heavyweight of the Denver Rocks. Ron was way more serious and talented, and I was getting a college degree, so he took over. Ron forged a relationship with Bill Daniels that would last for the remainder of their lives. I got a teaching and coaching job at Westminster High School in 1973 but still continued to box a bit. I began sparring with Lyle. I am sure my brain will shut down any day now because of this experience, but I hope it made me a little tougher and a lot more humble. I guess my best attributes as a fighter would have been my ability to take a punch. I was left handed, awkward, and not too mobile. If you were going to beat me though, you would be advised to hit me with a sledgehammer. I had seven pro fights: four in Vegas, one in Milwaukee, one in Denver on the Lyle-Ali exhibition under card and one in Nebraska. I compiled a 7-0 record against worse misfits than I beat as an amateur. I worked out with the fighters listed here three or four times a week for about twelve years. I probably had 250-plus rounds against Lyle and probably more against Leroy Jones. Looking back on this fact, it's a wonder this list is coherent at all.

2. Ron Lyle, Heavyweight.

I have already explained some of Lyle's exploits and his ability as a fighter is well chronicled. He didn't have a professional fight until he was 28 but rose to a highly ranked contender who fought the pants off of arguably the best heavyweight fighter of all time. I am proud to call Ron a friend. Much the same as George Foreman, Ron was perceived as aloof, unapproachable and hard-headed. In my dealings with him almost from the day I met him just the opposite was true. I think the same was true in George Foreman's case. I sparred with big George when he trained in Denver prior to going to Mexico City to be in the Olympics. In public, he was like Ron: perceived as a hardhead. He was very serious in the gym with his work but not nasty at all. Both were playful and talkative when the work was done. If Ron hit and hurt a sparring partner during a workout, he would be concerned about his health and never treat a sparring partner with disrespect. Because of his late start in boxing Ronnie's work ethic was off the charts. He was a great athlete naturally, and he soaked up knowledge from Bobby, and obviously it paid off. Ron's best quality strictly as a fighter was the fact that if he tagged an opponent with a left hook or a straight right hand, the fight was over. He is probably one of the top ten punchers of all time in the heavyweight division. He was also very adept at avoiding being hit. He fought a lot like Sonny Liston but had better feet. He never made sweeping adjustments either punching or slipping punches. All of Ronnie's punches were short and swift. Throughout boxing, almost all great hitters threw punches short distances and Ronnie was no exception. He has to rank very high when talking about great punchers in boxing. Everybody who is a boxing fan can recall his classic fight with Foreman but I always thought the better fight was his tussle with Earnie Shavers. When speaking about punchers among those who really know about the fight game, Earnie's name is revered. His knock out percentage is the highest of any fighter, ever! At one time he was 52-2 and all 52 victories were KOs. They fought at the Coliseum after Ron's loss to another great, although small, heavyweight: Jerry Quarry. Thinking about the heavyweights in the game at the time, from Sonny Liston to Larry Holmes ascending to the title, I can't believe the quality of fighters in this time period (late 60s to mid 80s). I can think of 15 to 20 fighters who could've beat all the heavyweight champions of today. Ron Lyle would certainly be one of them. Another great attribute of Ron Lyle was his focus. Most great athletes or performers have an uncanny ability to block out distractions when preparing to compete. Ron was an ace at this. A stroke of good fortune for Ronnie was his being discovered by Bill Daniels. Bill was a rare person in my opinion. He acquired great wealth but remained down to earth. He also loved boxing. I believe Ron made a critical mistake when he and his brother broke away from Bill to pursue fights on their own but it didn't really affect how they felt about one another. They were close until the day Bill passed away. Of all the fighters in our stable, Ron made the most money and attained a well-deserved stature of invincibility. Ronnie lives in Denver and trains fighters at the Red Shield Center.

1. Leroy Jones, Heavyweight.

The "other" heavyweight in our stable was a transplanted southern lad by the name of Leroy Jones. He was "recruited" by Bobby who saw him fight at the National Golden Gloves Tournament in Chicago in 1974. He was 6-foot-5 and weighed 265 lbs. He was playing football at Grambling at the time and was a great athlete. He came to Denver and began working with Bobby. This obviously led to Leroy working out with Ron. I will state right now that Leroy Jones could have been the heavyweight champion and held the title for sometime if he had focused and trained like Ron Lyle. He was young (23) when he came to Denver, but was a complete natural in a lot of aspects of boxing. He was huge, strong, very tough, and had great speed in his hands and feet. The only guy that never got wobbled by Lyle in countless rounds of sparring was Leroy. He had 34 pro fights after a very brief amateur stint and lost only one. He was very much a "carbon copy" of Larry Holmes in size, style, and punching ability. Larry Holmes is known for having one of the best jabs ever. Leroy's was better. He had longer arms and was faster than Larry Holmes. Leroy's negative characteristics were what all of us at the time knew would beat him. He hated to train. He also loved to eat. He was a gregarious soul who loved to have a good time and in most instances, he was not physically prepared to beat great fighters. At the outset I stated Leroy could have been special if his work ethic matched his physical gifts. Ron would tell you today that Leroy was better than him—if he worked. Many people in all walks of life have been afflicted with Leroy's disease. Being lazy. He was and is a great guy who I believe didn't achieve all he could but fought for the heavyweight crown. Even with his lack of training he still only lost one fight to Larry Holmes. That was no disgrace at all. Leroy is living in California, drives a big rig and is doing well.

A final note:

Bobby Lewis passed away in 1993. All of the people written about, inclusive of Bill Daniels, were present for his funeral. That was the last time I saw these guys all in one place. Outside of my own family, it was a special gathering of probably my favorite people I have ever known.

Irv's Top 10 College Football Games

Two of my favorite games involved CU. Who can forget 'em?

10. Jan. 1, 1994.

Florida State 18, Nebraska 16. Orange Bowl. A tight game. I admit there's some satisfaction in seeing the Huskers get beat.

9. November 20, 1982.

California 25, Stanford 20. Cal's five lateral passes on the final kickoff return stunned everyone for the win. The Stanford marching band was celebrating a Cardinal "victory" in the end zone. Oops.

8. January 2, 1984.

Orange Bowl. Miami 31, Nebraska 30. Miami got its first national title. Classic example of the "fumblerooskie" in this game. Not as satisfying to see the Huskers get beat, though.

7. October 6, 1990.

Colorado 33, Missouri 31. The famous "Fifth Down" game. With the extra play, CU QB Charles Johnson got the ball across the plane of the goal line. Some fans in Missouri disagree.

6. September 24, 1994.

Colorado 27, Michigan 26. Michael Westbrook catches Kordell Stewart's Hail Mary for the miracle.

5. December 2, 1995.

Army 14, Navy 13. Coulda woulda shoulda kicked that field goal, Navy.

4. January 3, 2003.

Ohio State 31, Miami 24. Two overtimes. Two well-matched teams. Football heaven.

3. October 15, 2005.

Southern California 34, Notre Dame 31. The Bush Push. Trojans win. Again.

2. January 4, 2006.

Texas 41, Southern California 38. Rose Bowl. Vince Young stole the spotlight from a team that had basked in it for a 34-game winning streak.

1. December 29, 2006.

Texas Tech 44, Minnesota 41. Insight Bowl. What a comeback—the Red Raiders repaired a 31-point deficit.

I've picked the five best bowl appearances by the University of Colorado, plus the five best by Air Force.

University of Colorado

5. 1938 Cotton Bowl.
CU loses to Rice 28-14. Buffs first Bowl team, featuring future Supreme Court Justice Byron "Whizzer" White.

4. 1971 Blue Bonnet Bowl.
CU defeats Houston 29-17. Eddie Crowder's best team. Buffs finished third nationally behind Nebraska and Oklahoma.

3. 1994 Fiesta Bowl.
CU beats Notre Dame in Bill McCartney's last game as head coach.

2. 1989 Orange Bowl.
CU loses to Notre Dame 21-6. Buffs lose shot at National title to one of Lou Holtz's best teams.

1. 1990 Orange Bowl.
CU defeats Notre Dame 10-9 to win the National title. Charles Johnson comes off the bench to quarterback CU over the Irish and win MVP.

Air Force

5. 1998 Oahu Bowl.
AFA defeats Washington 45-25. Another of Fisher DeBerry's best teams.

4. 1990 Liberty Bowl.
AFA defeats Ohio State 23-11. Falcons embarrass Buckeyes behind quarterback Rob Perez.

3. 1985 Blue Bonnet Bowl.
AFA beats Texas 24-16. Air Force's BEST EVER team. But for a fluke loss to BYU, Falcons probably played for the mythical National title.

2. 1970 Sugar Bowl.
AFA loses 34-13 to Tennessee. One of AFA's best ever teams, beat Missouri and Stanford's Rose Bowl team featuring Jim Plunkett.

1. 1958 Cotton Bowl.
AFA ties TCU 0-0. Falcons, playing in their first Bowl game, had not yet graduated their first senior class.

We asked our listeners to name the best college football coach ever. Here's the consensus dozen all-time best.

12. Ara Parseghian.

Notre Dame. Record: 95-17-4. Win: 83 percent. National Titles: 2.

11. Darrel Royal.

Texas. Record: 167-47-5. Win: 74 percent. National Championships: 3. Southwest Conference Titles: 11.

10. John Robinson.

USC. Record: 132-77-4. Win: 62 percent. National Titles: 1. Years Coaching: 18. Bowl Appearances: 9.

9. Barry Switzer.

Oklahoma. Record: 157-29-4. Win: 83 percent. National Titles: 3. Conference Titles: 12. Years Coaching: 16. Bowl Appearances: 13.

8. Bo Schembechler.

Michigan. Record: 234-65-8. Win: 76 percent. National Titles: 0. Conference Titles: 12 Big Ten. Years Coaching: 27. Bowl Appearances: 17.

7. Woody Hayes.

Ohio State. Record: 238-72-10. Win: 76 percent. National Titles: 3. Conference Titles: 13 Big Ten. Years Coaching: 28. Bowl Appearances: 17.

6. Lou Holtz.

Notre Dame. Record: 249-132-7. Win: 64 percent. National Titles: 1. Years Coaching: 33. Bowl Appearances: 22.

5. Tom Osbourne.

Nebraska. Record: 255-49-3. Win: 83 percent. National Titles: 3. Conference Titles: 13. Years Coaching: 24. Bowl Appearances: 17.

4. Paul "Bear" Bryant.

Alabama. Record: 323-85-17. Win: 76 percent. National Titles: 3. Conference Titles: 15 Sec. Years Coaching: 38. Bowl Appearances: 29.

3. Joe Paterno.

Penn State. Record: 365-121-3. Win: 75 percent. National Titles: 2. Conference Titles: 2 Big Ten. Years Coaching: 42. Bowl Appearances: 33.

2. Bobby Bowden.

Florida State. Record: 367-113-4. Win: 76 percent. National Titles: 2. Conference Titles: 12 ACC. Years Coaching: 41. Bowl Appearances: 21.

1. Eddie Robinson.

Grambling. Record: 408-165-15. Win: 69 percent. National Titles: 1. Conference Titles: 17. Years Coaching: 56.

In the 1970s, I was the head baseball coach and an assistant football coach at CU. Here's a list—in no particular order—of some of the best of the 70s. All went on to earn a living in the pros.

Dan Stavely.
Varsity football, 1972. This was the first year freshmen were eligible to play varsity ball, and four who started out on the freshman team who were called up became stars and played in the NFL. Dan had never lost a freshman game. I was in charge, and the team went 3-1, losing to Nebraska.

Billy Waddy.
A dangerous kick-returner who was sixth on the all-time CU ledger in all-purpose yards. Played eight years in the NFL.

Mike Spivy.
He started out at linebacker and moved to cornerback. He had amazing speed and played for the Chicago Bears. He still lives in the Denver area.

Leon White.
He excelled at three different positions on the offensive line. He played in the NFL then went on to fame as a pro wrestler.

Don Hasselback.
The tight end actually played in one game vs. Dodge City JUCO. He was called up to the varsity and made all Big Eight. He played in the NFL. His son Matt is the quarterback for the Seattle Seahawks.

Dudley "Bo" Mitchell.
Basketball. Tremendous outside shooter for Sox Walseth. He was all Big Eight in baseball, too. He got to AA in the Cardinal Farm Chain. He currently lives in Denver and runs Garth Brooks' youth foundation. His dad Dale was a career 300-hitter in the Big Leagues.

Jay Howell.
From Fairview High School, he was a solid pitcher for three years, then signed with Cincinnati. He was with several Big League teams as a quality reliever.

Bobby Anderson.
Anderson is one of only three CU football players to have their number retired. Joe Romig and Byron White are the others. He set 18 records at CU. He played six seasons in the NFL. He also had a long career as a broadcaster.

John Stearns.
"Bad Dude" Football and baseball. Stearns was a feared hitter who earned first-team All-Big Eight honors his senior season, the same year he was voted the Buffs' most valuable player. He starred on the great 1971 team, and ended his football career with 16 interceptions. He was also a great baseball player at Colorado and played 10 seasons in the majors with the New York Mets, and he is still coaching in professional baseball.

Stan Brock.

He was a first-team All-American as a senior in 1979. He was also most outstanding lineman that year. Brock played in 112 consecutive games in the NFL, and 16 seasons. He currently is head coach at Army.

Herb Orvis and Bud Mangrum.

These two tough guys came to CU after the service, and they could really play on the defensive end.

Cullen Bryant.

From Colorado Springs, he was a big bruising cornerback who played a running back for years with the Rams in the NFL.

Dave Logan.

One of the greatest athletes of all time at Colorado. He was drafted professionally in football, basketball (out of college) and baseball (out of high school). He played in the NFL for nine years. He is now a championship-winning high school coach and sports broadcaster.

J.V. Cain.

He was a tight end, a lot like Shannon Sharpe in his style. He had a great career going with St. Louis. He died way too early.

Cliff Branch.

He had sprinter speed. He returned six punts and two kickoffs for touchdowns in the span of two seasons. He was the team's MVP in 1971. That team was one of the best ever at CU. Branch played 14 seasons in the NFL, and has three Super Bowl rings.

Troy Archer.

Archer ended his career as a Buffalo with 14 sacks. He played three seasons in the NFL before he died in a car accident in 1979.

Laval Short.

A top interior lineman. Two years in the NFL.

CU had three 1,000-point scorers and all went on to play in the NBA.

Cliff Meeley.

He was winding up his career in 1971 and he was a scoring machine. He set a Big Eight record with 427 points.

Scott Wedman.

He was a walk-on from Mullen and ended up the 16th all-time scorer in CU history. Kansas City Royals drafted him in the first round. He is in the Colorado Sports Hall of Fame.

Jim Creighton.

From North High School. He is number 22 on the all-time scoring list. He played in the NBA with Atlanta.

Note: Bill McCartney, Buffs head coach from 1982 to 1994, rebuilt the University of Colorado football program. In just seven years, he took the team from a ranking of 110th in the nation to number one. In 1986, he coached the Buffs to their first win over Nebraska in more than 20 years. In 1990, the Buffs won the Orange Bowl, defeating Notre Dame—the team that had defeated the Buffs the previous year. Bill is one of the most inspirational people in Colorado sports. He founded a ministry called Promise Keepers, which some people found controversial. He retired from coaching and continues to pursue his calling. We asked him to name some of his (many) notable CU players, in no particular order.

Darien Hagen.

His greatest strength was his instinct. He could dart into something and make things happen.

Eric Bienemy.

Five-foot six, 190 pounds and nine years in the NFL. He had heart. He was the most competitive guy I ever coached.

Matt Lepsis.

In the NFL longer than anybody I coached. In High School he was number two in the nation in the discus. That will tell you something. I played him at tight end to get everyone else involved.

Alfred Williams.

"Race Horse." They couldn't block him coming off the edge.

Charles Johnson.

The wide out was the most difficult to defend. Strong endurance.

Koy Detmer.

Single biggest difference-maker. As a 160-pound freshman, he went into the Minnesota game and saved the day. Nine years in the NFL.

It's one of the most memorable officiating mistakes in the history of Colorado sports. It helped the University of Colorado Buffaloes to a victory over the Missouri Tigers in a football game on October 6, 1990. The Buffs were driving, down 31-27 in the final minutes of the game. QB Charles S. Johnson passed to tight end Jon Boman, who got the first down but fell before he could reach the end zone. The Buffs should have had four downs after that, but they got five. Let's count 'em.

1. First Down.
Johnson spikes the ball to stop the clock.

2. Second Down.
Eric Bieniemy, CU's all-time leader in rushing, is held out of the end zone on a run. The Buffs call their last timeout.

3. Third Down.
Same play as the last. Bieniemy is stopped short of the goal line.

4. Fourth Down.
Johnson spikes the ball, stopping the clock with two seconds remaining. He and officials are unaware that it's fourth down.

5. Fifth Down.
Johnson makes it across the goal line by a whisker, if that. After review, the officials call it a touchdown. By this time, officials are made aware of the extra down. Still, the Buffs win by two, 33 to 31. The Big Eight reviews the result and upholds the Buff's victory. Seven officials are suspended indefinitely.

Top College Football Teams :: Pat Forde

Note: Pat Forde is a senior writer for ESPN.com. His weekly column is called "The Forde Yard Dash." Pat grew up in Colorado Springs and played football for Gary Barnett at Air Force Academy High School. He covers a top team each week. Here are his picks of the four best college football teams of all time.

4. Miami 2001–2002.

Larry Goken set the bar too high and it cost him down the road.

3. USC 2004.

Pete may not have had it all in the NFL, but his Trojans are a dynasty.

2. USC 2005.

Pete Carroll appeared to have the overall winner until Young took over on the last drive.

1. Texas 2005.

Featuring the amazing Vince Young. Mack Brown wins his National Championship.

A Nod to the Buckeyes :: Tom Kensler

Note: *Denver Post* staff writer Tom Kensler was voted the 2007 Colorado sportswriter of the year. He joined the paper in 1989 and covers CU sports. A graduate of the Ohio State University, he lists his Five Top Ohio State teams.

5. 1975 (11-1).

Led by a backfield of tailback Archie Griffin, fullback Pete Johnson, quarterback Cornelius Greene and wingback Brian Baschnagel, Buckeyes roll through the regular season but are surprised 23-10 in the Rose Bowl by a UCLA team that fell 41-20 to the Buckeyes during the regular season.

4. 1961 (8-0-1).

An opening game tie to TCU ultimately costs Buckeyes an unbeaten season but the Football Writers Association of America names Ohio State the national championship. A blue-chip trio of running backs Matt Snell, Bob Ferguson and Paul Warfield leads the Buckeyes.

3. 1954 (10-0).

Coaching legend Woody Hayes wins the national championship in his fourth season in Columbus with talented squad led by running back Howard "Hopalong" Cassady, who would win the Heisman Trophy the next season, and sophomore lineman Jim Parker, a future Pro Football Hall of Famer.

2. 2002 (14-0).

Led by a punishing defense and ball-control offense, Buckeyes complete a magical unde-feated season with a 31-24 double-overtime win over Miami (Fla.) in the BCS national championship game at the Fiesta Bowl. OSU, an 11 1/2 point underdog, ends Hurricanes' 34-game winning streak.

1. 1968 (10-0).

Led by super sophs Rex Kern, Jack Tatum, Jim Stillwagon and John Brockington, Buckeyes earned the national championship with a win over O.J. Simpson-led Southern Cal in the Rose Bowl.

Note: Troy is Associate Athletic Director For Communications at the U.S. Air Force Academy in Colorado Springs. He lists the top 10 Air Force athletes of all time.

10. Beau Morgan, 1997.

All-American in 1996 as an all-purpose player. Finished 10th in the Heisman Trophy voting in 1996 as a senior. First player in NCAA history to rush and pass for over 1,000 yards—each, twice. AF career record holder with 594 carries. School-record with 1,494 yards rushing in 1996. 42 career rushing touchdowns, which is an AF record.

9. Eric Ehn, 2008.

Most celebrated player in AF program history. Finalist for the 2007 Hobey Baker Award as the nation's top player. First-team All-American, led the Falcons to their first NCAA hockey tournament and the Atlantic Hockey Conference tournament championship. Led the nation in scoring as a junior.

8. Callie Calhoun, 1991.

Air Force head football coach Troy Calhoun's younger sister. Five-time NCAA Division II track and field national champion (3,000 meters, 5,000 meters, 10,000 meters.) 1990 NCAA Division II cross country national champion. Eight-time All-American in track and three-time All-American in cross country. Also an academic All-American.

7. Dana Pounds, 2005.

Two-time NCAA track and field champion in the javelin. School and MWC record holder in the javelin. Recruited as a women's basketball player. Decided to leave the team and go out for track. Had never thrown the javelin in her life before her freshman year in track. Currently in the Air Force World Class Athlete Program and in training for the 2008 Olympic Games. First Air Force Academy female Division I All-American.

6. Jason Brown, 2006.

Played both football and baseball. Was the team's top pitcher in baseball as a freshman. Recorded 49 catches for 879 yards in football as a senior in 2005. Recorded those statistics in football with two different quarterbacks splitting time.

5. Dee Dowis, 1990.

Finished sixth in the Heisman Trophy voting in 1989 as a senior. Fourth player in NCAA history to rush and pass for over a 1,000 yards each in a single season. School records with 249 yards and six touchdowns vs. SDSU in 1989. Single-digit golf handicap (about a 4) while at the Academy.

4. Carlton McDonald, 1993.

Consensus All-American in 1992 as a senior. Once blocked three kicks in one game and was the Academy record-holder with nine career blocks. Second all-time in AF history with 16 career interceptions. Runner up for the Thorpe Award as a senior. Projected first-round draft pick, but went to pilot training.

3. Raymond Dudley, 1990.
Two-time honorable mention All-American. Only player in school history to lead the team in scoring all four years. All-time leading scorer in AF history with 2,178 points. Had a 40 inch vertical leap.

2. Chad Hennings, 1988.
1987 Outland Trophy Winner and consensus All-American. Inducted into the College Football Hall of Fame. WAC player of the decade for the 1980s. Most celebrated football player in AF history.

1. Mike Thiessen, 2001.
Two-time All-American baseball player. MWC Football conference offensive player of the year in 2000. Only player in school history to rush for 100 yards and throw for 200 yards in a game (vs. Fresno State in 2000 Silicon Valley Bowl). Would play in a baseball game and practice football in the same day during the spring.

DU Football Memories

One of the first football stadiums in the area was located at Asbury Avenue and South Race Street in Denver. Built in 1926, it was home to the University of Denver Pioneers Football team. Later, it was the site of early Broncos exhibition games. The Pioneers ended their football program in the 1960s, and the stadium was torn down in 1971. All that remains are great football memories. There was a time when the DU vs. CU game was a must-see at Thanksgiving. Here are some top names from the glory days of DU football.

10. Rusty Fairly.
QB. The "Mad Magician." Mr. Excitement. You never knew what he was going to do.

9. Tom Hugo.
The guy from Hawaii was a center who could get out on the middle linebacker.

8. Fred Tesone.
Great speed; could get outside.

7. Ed Stewart.
A tough tackle from Annunciation.

6. Mike Jurich.
Never saw him take a play off.

5. Dick Yates.
A guard who played both ways. At 150 pounds, he was tough.

4. Greg Browning.
Tough end who played both ways.

3. Johnny Karamigios.
"The Galloping Greek from Cherry Creek." Could really run off tackle.

2. Ernie Pitts.
A great receiver who was also a good center fielder.

1. Sam "The Rifle" Etcheverry.
Great touch. The most famous Pioneer, he was from Carlsbad, New Mexico. He played at DU from 1949-1951 and set all the passing records. He was the MVP of the CFL in 1954, threw for 3,610, eclipsing the then-record in the NFL set by "Slingin'" Sammy Baugh. Etcheverry later played QB in the NFL for the Cardinals. He also played in Canada for the Montreal Allouettes.

Irv's Favorite UNC Bears

The University of Northern Colorado in Greeley was the third school founded in the relatively new State of Colorado, way back in 1889. They started playing football in 1893. Never had much success. The most games the school ever won in a season was six. They did it twice—once in 1957, and once in 1963. Things changed in 1966 when Bob Blasi took over. In 18 years he was 107-71-3 and won six RMAC championships. In 1969 they went 10-0. The golden years started in 1989 when Joe Glenn took over. What a run. In 10 years he went 98-35 and his win percentage was 73 percent. In 1996 the Bears went 12-3 and won the Division II National championship, beating Carson Newman. The following year, UNC repeated going 13-2 beating New Haven for the championship. Joe moved onto Montana and had the same kind of success. He is currently the head coach at the University of Wyoming. Here are my top 10 players ever at UNC.

10. Dave Stalls.
Really came on his senior year and was drafted in the seventh round by the Dallas Cowboys, and was a solid contributor.

9. Billy Holmes.
During the championship years, Billy was amazing. He rushed for 1,593 yards in 1996 and 1,587 yards in 1997. When it was on the line, Billy was the go-to guy.

8. Tony Ramirez.
A consensus two-time All-American in 1995 and 1996. Drafted in the sixth round by Detroit. Flawless form.

7. Bill Kenney.
Here's a guy who came on late. He was a tight end, moved to quarterback and was a starter for the Kansas City Chiefs. He would start reading the defense when the huddle broke.

6. Frank Wainright.
A tight end who was an All-American in 1990. He could block and catch. He was drafted in the sixth round, number 210, by the Saints; then played for Baltimore.

5. Adam Mathews.
Is the third all-time leading rusher in UNC history. What a year he had in 2003. He rushed for 1,653 yards, scored 126 points, and rushed for 279 yards vs. Adams State. He played for the Hamburg Sea Devils. His father Bo played at CU and was the fifth pick overall in the draft.

4. Reed Doughty.
Was a real force in the secondary. He played 2002-2005. He would knock your head off. He's in the record books for interceptions and fumble recoveries. He was drafted in the sixth round by Washington. He is still active.

3. Vincent Jackson.

Six-foot-seven. The guy who was supposed to play hoops turned into a great wideout at UNC; two-time all-conference selection. Associated Press All-American. He was drafted in the second round by the Chargers and has already established himself in the NFL.

2. Cort McGuffey.

Threw 93 touchdown passes from 1996-1999 for an incredible 8,781 yards. His total offense was 9,362 yards. Cort really benefited from having Kay Dalton who had a ton of experience in college and the pros. He played pro ball with the New York/New Jersey Hitmen.

1. Aaron Smith.

Fifty-nine Bears have played pro football. Smith is the best one, competing for the Steelers. He does just what he did at UNC – sack the quarterback. He had 55 sacks from 1995-1998.

UNC Trivia Bonus:

4.

The worst year the Bears ever had been 1949. They were 0-8 and lost to Wyoming 103-0.

3.

In 1937 Elmo Cromer scored 26 points vs. Montana State. He was tough; spent 18 months in a Nazi concentration camp. Now deceased. He was a very successful coach at Eaton.

2.

In 1969 Ben Pyatt led the Bears in rushing. His son Brad was a wideout in 2002 and went to run back punts for Indianapolis. Now in Arena Ball with the Colorado Crush.

1.

Mike Wolford led the Bears in rushing in 1966. He coached football at Cherry Creek and won five state titles in 10 years.

Football has been played at Colorado State University in Fort Collins for more than 115 seasons. In 1992, Sonny Lubick became the head coach and turned the program into a success. The program was considered a dead-end until Sonny took over. Sonny guided the Rams to six conference titles and nine bowl appearances. He did an amazing job. The school hadn't had a winning season since the early fifties under Bob Davis. Many had tried—like Tuffy Mullison, Mike Lude, Jerry Wampfler and Earl Bruce. Before Sonny's arrival, the Rams had played in two post-season games in school history. He was selected national coach of the year in 1994 by *Sports Illustrated.* That year, which was Sonny's second season in Fort Collins, the Rams pulled off a monumental upset against No. 4-ranked Arizona in Tucson, and beat two other top-25 teams. In 1998, at (heavily favored) Michigan State, CSU won 23-16. They took it to 19th-ranked Missouri in the 1997 Holiday Bowl. They played unbelievable games against Air Force and BYU. They've been fun and entertaining throughout. More than anything, Sonny is a marvelous person—he treats people right. In 2007, the school replaced Sonny with Steve Fairchild—a decision that stirred up a lot of controversy. Fort Collins and the state of Colorado owe Sonny a great debt. He's one of my favorite Rams. Here's a list of 10 more.

10. Brady Smith.
He would put the quarterback on his back. He did the same thing professionally with the Atlanta Falcons.

9. Erik Pears.
The kid from Kennedy made huge strides and now is a fixture with the Broncos.

8. David Anderson.
I never saw him drop a pass, and he'd go across the middle.

7. Clark Haggans.
His first step as a down-lineman got my attention. From the get go he's done the same thing with the Steelers.

6. Cecil Sapp.
He was a real gamer for Sonny and has played running back, fullback and special teams for the Broncos since 2003.

5. Keli McGregor.
From Lakewood High School. Big guy, 6-foot-7. Safetys couldn't handle him. He was all-league and played for two teams in the NFL. Now president of the Colorado Rockies. His dad Brian played in the Canadian league and was a successful coach at Arvada West.

4. Bradlee Van Pelt.
Transferred from Michigan State. Everybody wanted to play him on defense. He wanted to be a quarterback. Sonny relented—he was the league's MVP.

3. Greg Myers.

From Little Windsor, Colorado. He was a dominating safety for the Rams. He played in the NFL with Cincinnati.

2. Kevin McDougal.

The running back from Arvada West gave you a go every snap. Sonny Lubick came very close to moving him to safety. That would have been tragic.

1. Thurman "Fum" McGraw.

No one was more loyal to his school than Fum. A great player and a solid athletic director. He was the first pro lineman I saw who would pursue when he played with the Detroit Lions.

Colorado School of Mines in Golden is known for brains, not athletes. Not that the two are mutually exclusive—not always, anyway. It's one of the toughest schools in America. You get a degree from there, and you get a great job. The school teaches you to work hard and solve problems—it's a public research university devoted to engineering and applied science. They've been playing football since 1888. A guy played if he had time. It's as simple as that: academics first. The school had two cheers that have come down through the ages: "That's all right, that's okay, you'll work for us one day." And, "Mines Raw, Mines Raw, how's yours?" The football team never won more than six games in a row. Things changed in 2000 when Bob Stitt became the head coach. He was 2-8 his first year. He hasn't had a losing year since. His record is 51 and 40. In 2004 they went 12-1 and won the tough RMAC League title and got to the semi-finals in NCAA Division II. Here are three Orediggers who come to mind when we think about Mines football.

3. Lloyd Madden.

He scored 23 touchdowns in 1939. He's in the Colorado Sports Hall of Fame. He played one year in the NFL, for the Chicago Cardinals in 1940.

2. Dutch Clark.

The NFL Hall of Famer. He coached the Orediggers for one year in 1933. In 1929, he played for Colorado College and was the football player from that school to be named All-America. He played professionally for the Portsmouth Spartans in 1931 season, but left after just two seasons to become the head coach at Mines. He went back to the pros in 1934, to the Detroit Lions. He set a longstanding rushing record, plus kicked field goals and extra points. Later, he coached the Lions and the Cleveland Rams.

1. Chad Friehauf.

In 2004, he helped the team to its first conference football title since 1958. The quarterback was named the 2004 Division II National Player of the Year. Friehauf had 5,363 yards total offense in 2004, and 412.5 total offensive yards per game, setting NCAA II records. He won the Harlon Hill Trophy (the Division II equivalent of the Heisman Trophy) and scads of additional honors. He's the all-time school-record setter in attempts, completions, passing yards and touchdowns. He signed a free agent contract with the Denver Broncos following the 2005 NFL Draft. But he didn't stay long. He went back to basketball, now playing for Mines as he pursues another undergraduate degree.

Listed by decade.

2000s

Jason Smith.
CSU. Jason was the MWC Freshman of the Year. Great leaper. Great speed. Was a first round pick in the NBA Draft by Philadelphia.

David Harrison.
CU. Best is ahead. Great skills. Now with the Indiana Pacers.

1990s

Donnie Boyce.
CU. Colorado's all-time leading scorer, with 1,995 career points. Was drafted by Atlanta. Had a promising NBA career cut short by a broken leg.

Demarcus Anzures.
Metro State. All-time leader in steals, three-point field goals and minutes played. His dad Fred was pretty good at CSU.

Chauncey Billups.
CU. One of the premier guards in CU history. Was on campus two years and earned All-American Honors. Then became a star in the pros.

1980s

Jay Humphries.
CU. All-time leader in steals. Selected to the All-American Team.

Pat Durham.
CSU. Monster on the boards. All-time leading Ram rebounder.

Shaun Vandiver.
CU. Big guy. Solid game. 18th pick overall by the Golden State Warriors.

1970s

Scott Wedman.
CU. A walk-on from Mullen. Ended up as a great scorer who was a first-round pick of the Kansas City Royals.

Cliff Meely.
CU. A scoring machine. A complete player. Named to several All-American teams as a junior and senior.

Dale Schlueter.
CSU. Solid guy. Played a long time in the NBA.

1960s

William Green.
Colorado A&M. The best player in Rams history. The quiet man from Alabama was a force in the paint.

Byron Beck.
DU. He was so good on the hilltop and in the pros with the Denver Nuggets. They retired his number.

Ken Charlton.
CU. Battled knee injuries during his career. Was named to the All-American Team in 1963. He was pretty good in the classroom—an Academic All-American.

Harry Hollines.
DU. This left-hander is the best outside shooter ever at DU. In a class with Pat Frink.

Pat Frink.
Pure shooter. Averaged 18 points per game and was a teammate of Oscar Robertson of the Cincinnati Royals.

1950s

Stan Albert.
Colorado A&M. All-Conference selection and the best six-foot rebounder in the nation.

Hal Kinard.
Colorado A&M. A great defender who had an unstoppable fade-away jumper.

Bob Beckel.
Air Force Academy. The greatest scorer in school history. Later became the commandant of the Academy.

Burdette Haldorson.
CU. Unstoppable in 1955. Led the Big Seven in scoring. Played later for Phillips 66. He represented our country twice in the Olympics.

1940s

Vince Boryla.
Started out at Notre Dame and came here in the service. He stayed and played at DU and was an All-American.

Robert Doll.
Big play man for Frosty Cox at CU. Earned All-American honors. He was a great rebounder and controlled the paint. Went on to play for the Boston Celtics.

Note: Ryan Thornburn is a solid columnist for the Boulder *Daily Camera*. He's from Wyoming. He went to the university and is extremely loyal. Ryan lists his top 10 athletes from the University of Wyoming.

10. Marcus Harris.

Football playmaker, 1993-1996. Won the Biletnikoff Trophy as the nation's top receiver in 1996. He had three consecutive 1,400-yard seasons. Drafted by the Detroit Lions.

9. Jim Kiick.

Football, 1965-67. Wyoming's leading rusher for three consecutive seasons. Helped lead the team to the 1968 Sugar Bowl. He was on the undefeated 1972 Miami Dolphins team with Larry Csonka. The Kiick/Csonka duo was called "Butch Cassidy and the Sundance Kid." Helped take Miami to three Super Bowls.

8. Jay Novacek.

Two sport All-American in football and track, 1982-84. As a tight end, he had 83 career receptions for 1,536 yards and 10 touchdowns. Had a great run with the Dallas Cowboys; was part of the 1993 Super Bowl Champion team.

7. Greg Brock.

Baseball, 1976-1979. One of Wyoming's best hitters. Three-year starter with the Dodgers.

6. Dick Ballinger.

Wrestling, 1958-60. The only wrestler at Wyoming to win a NCAA championship. Earned All-American three times.

5. Charles "Tub" Bradley.

Basketball, 1979-81. One of the greatest and most exciting athletes. He finished as the second leading scorer in Cowboy history with 1,744 points. Drafted in the first round by the Celtics.

4. Theo Ratliff.

Basketball, 1992-95. Our best shot blocker. Had 425 career blocks, which was one of this highest in NCAA history. Owned the glass. Successful pro. Picked in the first round by the Pistons.

3. Flynn Robinson.

Basketball, 1963-65. Greatest range ever in hoops. He broke every major Wyoming basketball record except rebounding. Played in the NBA for the Bucks and the Lakers.

2. Kenny Sailors.

Basketball, 1941-46. He's the guy who invented the Jump Shot, a huge contribution to the sport. Earned All-American three times. Played in the pros.

1. Fennis Dembo.

Basketball, 1985-88. People's choice. Finished as Wyoming's all-time scoring leader with 2,311 points. Was also the leader in rebounding, with 954. The first Wyoming basketball player ever to grace the cover of Sports Illustrated. Played for the Pistons on their 1989 championship team.

Some others who could push to get in the top 10:

Eddie Talboom.

Football.

Bill Garnett.

Basketball.

Jerry Hill.

Football.

The Best Game Ever :: Charlie Brown

Note: Charlie Brown is probably the best-known member of Denver City Council. He's always in the papers with great quotes and comments. He also served in the Colorado Legislature for a while. He's a proud graduate of the University of Wyoming (1969, Political Science.) Here he lists memorable moments from Wyoming's "Best Game Ever," the 2004 Las Vegas Bowl.

4. Joe Glenn stood in the lobby of the Golden Nugget wearing a grin as wide as the open range of Wyoming, greeting Cowboy football fans as they checked into the downtown Las Vegas hotel.

It was a moment almost as rare as the huge golden nugget displayed in a bullet- proof glass case, well guarded a few feet away in the corner of the lobby. Two-year football Head Coach Glenn had taken a dismal program with just five victories over the three previous seasons, and got here with a 7- 5 record.

3. Playing in the 2004 Las Vegas Bowl—in one of the driest states in the union—was appropriate.

Wyoming had a 38-year drought of post-season bowl victories. Picked last in the Mountain West Conference, Wyoming wasn't expected to do much that season, much less make a bowl appearance. Up against a cocky UCLA team, the Cowboys were 12-point underdogs, and weren't expected to make much of a showing. In fact, according to the UCLA student newspaper, the Bruins were embarrassed to have to play the unheralded Cowboys. "Where is Wyoming?" the headlines screamed, mocking the rural cowboy state, the university and the team. The Wyoming players knew they were getting no respect when, at the pre-game luncheon, some UCLA players refused to shake hands.

2. On a bitter cold night the Cowboys "Cowboyed Up" and rallied from 11 points down in the fourth quarter to stun the UCLA cityslickers.

Quarterback Corey Bramlet threw a hard pass over the middle that stuck like a tick in the hands of tight end John Woodkowski for a 12-yard touchdown with 57 seconds left. Wyoming won a 24-21 victory before a bowl-record, in-house crowd of 27,784 at Sam Boyd stadium. It was the Cowboys' first bowl victory since a 28-20 win over Florida State in the 1966 Sun Bowl.

1. Back at the Golden Nugget, Cowboy fans celebrated the end of the bowl drought.

Impromptu shouts of the familiar mantra from the school's fight song, "Powder River," answered by "Let'er Buck," ricocheted throughout the bar and casino until the wee hours of the morning. It is not often you go to Las Vegas and come away winners! It was the greatest collegiate game and festivities I have ever experienced. Go Pokes!

More fascinating stuff that most Broncos fans know but probably forgot. Listed in order of general relevance and overall benefit to humanity.

10. Tax brake.

Back in 1967, Denver-area voters rejected using tax dollars to build a new stadium for the Broncos. Opponents of public financing chanted, "Go, Broncos, Go . . . and good riddance." Funny how back-to-back Super Bowl championships can change the mood of the electorate.

9. Naming rights and wrongs.

In the early days, too many people were confusing Denver Bears Stadium with the home of the Chicago Bears. Locals wanted the stadium's name to reflect the city's nickname, the Mile High City, on account of our altitude being 5280 feet above sea level. In On November 21, 1968, Bears Stadium was officially renamed Mile High Stadium. Many years and many millions of dollars later, an investment management company based in Atlanta bought the naming rights to the Broncos' new home: INVESCO Field at Mile High. It opened in 2001.

8. Fumble-related suicide.

For decades, the Broncos were a national laughingstock, kind of like the Nuggets are today. The team suffered all kinds of humiliation. Broncos fans took it very, very personally. In a 1973 game against Chicago, the Broncos fumbled five times and lost the game. A Denver resident killed himself that night, saying in a suicide note, "I just can't stand their fumbling anymore."

7. Blackouts.

Remember TV blackouts? Wow, they used to rankle local fans. Home games were not broadcast on local TV. If you wanted to see the game, you had to buy a ticket and go sit in the stands. In 1973, the rule was relaxed. If a home game sold out 72 hours prior to kickoff, the game would be shown on local TV. Blackouts were meant to help the team build fans and make money, but they really rubbed a lot of people the wrong way.

6. Orange Monday.

Denver Mayor Bill McNichols declared Monday, October 22, 1973, "Orange Monday." On that day, Denver was in the national spotlight as Howard Cosell and Monday Night Football came to town for the first time ever. The Broncos played the Raiders. Jim Turner kicked a field goal to tie the game in the final seconds. There were no overtime periods back then. The game was hailed as a success for the Broncos, and voters soon stepped up to approve $25 million in bonds to improve the stadium.

5. Dirty Dozen.

Twelve Broncos players submitted a letter to then-owner Gerald Phipps asking that head coach John Ralston be fired. In 1976, the team went 9-5 but didn't make the playoffs. Many blamed Ralston. Ralston was let go. Ironically, the team would make it to the Super Bowl the next season with a team built mostly by Ralston.

4. Checkmate.
Orange Crush players liked to play chess. They said it helped them play better football. Barney Chavous, Rubin Carter and Tom Jackson were among the Broncos' notable chess afficianados.

3. Dallas connection.
Broncos QB Craig Morton wore number 7 before Elway. Morton had played for the Dallas Cowboys and led them to Super Bowl V, which the Cowboys lost. Morton led the Broncos to their first Super Bowl appearance, against the Dallas Cowboys. Morton's team lost again.

2. Orange Crush.
People remember the nickname, but they forget how good this defensive team was. The Orange Crush allowed only 148 points, and only 17 points in the fourth quarter, during the 1977 regular season.

1. Broncomania.
In 1977, the Broncos went 12-2 and made the playoffs. It's hard to describe the frenzied intensity of Denver fans during this time. People painted their houses, cars and children orange. Sales of Orange Crush soda went up ten thousand percent in Denver, and the manufacturer put out a special commemorative can. Everything was orange.

Note: Sideline reporter and announcer Brian Roth is a familiar voice on Comcast Entertainment Television (CET.) CET covers around 100 prep events in Colorado every year. Here are Brian's picks of top preps performances.

10. Andy Burns, Rocky Mountain Baseball.

Few around the state knew about Andy Burns and the Rocky Mountain baseball team before the 2007 state tournament. And when all was said and done, few could forget the performance by both. Burns and the Lobos dominated, going 5-0 in the double-elimination tournament, outscoring their opponents 55-15. Burns was named the MVP by hitting .600, with four homeruns and 12 RBI's. Burns will be a senior in 2008 and is expected to be a top four round draft pick in the June 2008 baseball draft.

9. Pierre Allen, Thomas Jefferson Basketball/Football.

At six-five and 225 pounds, he was a force in the paint for the Spartan basketball team. Allen was a beast on the glass, leading TJ to the 4A state championship in both his junior and senior seasons, earning tournament MVP honors both years. Allen was also an all-state defensive end for the Spartans football team. He earned a full ride scholarship to the University of Nebraska where he currently plays football.

8. Donnell Wells, Denver East Basketball.

A super-quick guard who burst on to the Colorado scene as a junior in 2006. A year later, he was leading the charge for Rudy Carey's Angels as they made a commanding run to a state title in March of 2007. Wells was by far the best player throughout the state tournament. He is currently playing for Trinidad State Junior College.

7. Evan Anundsen, Columbine Baseball.

Another high school pitcher who overpowered hitters. Low 90s fastball with great command and a sharp curve ball to go with it. Led the Rebels to the 2006 5A state championship and was named MVP of the state tournament. The Milwaukee Brewers selected Anundsen in the 4th round of the 2006 June amateur draft.

6. Anthony Capra, Arvada West Baseball.

An intimidating presence on the hill for the Wildcats. Capra was a lefty who had a fastball in the low 90s. He is still the only pitcher ever to throw a no hitter on CET when he struck out 16 in a shutout win over Chatfield in 2005. Went 7-1 with a 1.76 era at Wichita State last season.

5. Rachel Holloway, Smoky Hill Volleyball.

A dominant high school player who could do it all, from a devastating jump serve to a powerful attack at the net. Holloway is hands down the best all-around volleyball player CET has seen. She would leave high school early to enroll at the University of Nebraska where she led them to a National Championship as a freshmen setter in 2006.

4. Kendra Chandhoke, Heritage Soccer.

At Heritage High School, Chandhoke was one of the most dynamic high school soccer players in the state of Colorado. Chandhoke was a threat to score every time the ball touched her feet. She led Heritage to the state semifinals in both 2005 and 2006 and has played on many U.S. National teams in her career. Chandhoke is currently a forward for national power Portland, where she scored 10 goals helped lead the Pilots to the NCAA Quarterfinals in 2007 as true freshmen.

3. Melissa Jones, Legacy Basketball/Volleyball.

Perhaps the best female athlete seen in the state of Colorado since 2004. Along with being a powerful attacker in the sport of volleyball, she was widely considered the best basketball player in the state during the 2006-2007 season. Averaged 22 points, 10 rebounds, and 6 steals per game during her senior season. She received a full ride scholarship to play basketball at Baylor where she is in the starting lineup as a true freshman.

2. Abby Waner, Thunder Ridge Basketball.

Arguably the most decorated female athlete to ever come out of the state of Colorado. She led Thunder Ridge to three straight state championships and finished her senior season by averaging 32 points, 7.5 rebounds and 7 assists per game. Waner was named both the Gatorade and McDonald's national player of the year as a senior. She is perhaps the most competitive athlete covered by CET. She signed with Duke where she now leads the nationally ranked Blue Devils.

1. Matt Bouldin, Thunder Ridge Basketball.

The most talented guard to come out of the state of Colorado since George Washington's Chauncey Billups. Bouldin played four years of variety, helping the Grizzlies to a state championship as a freshman. As a sophomore and a junior, Bouldin led Thunder Ridge to state runner-up finishes. The six-five point guard averaged 25 points and 6.4 rebounds per game as a senior. He signed with Gonzaga and played in all 34 games as a true freshman and started the final 15 games.

Note: During his 40-some-odd-year career as a coach, Maurice "Stringy" Ervin led the Lions of Littleton High School to 12 state swimming titles. In 1988, he was named national coach of the year, and has been inducted into the National High School Coaches Hall of Fame. Stringy is a Littleton native. He graduated from LHS in 1960. Many don't know that he was a champion quarterback and a star pitcher for the Lions. He went to college at Fort Lewis and played football there, but suffered a knee injury that almost ended his entire athletic career. He started playing golf. He became a teacher, teaching phys ed and English, and he became a coach. The rest is a history of outstanding achievement. We asked Stringy to name some of the best names in swimming in Colorado.

Top Three Swimmers Coached by Stringy at Littleton HS:

3. Jack Taylor.
Florida.

2. Bob Patten.
SMU, All-American.

1. Sam Worden.
Stanford, All-American.

Top Male and Female Swimmers in the State:

1. Amy VanDyken.
Cherry Creek HS, CSU, Olympian.

1. Mark Dylla.
Heritage HS. Recently graduated. Now at the University of Georgia. The best ever.

Best Coaches:

2. Kirk Price and Eric Craven.
Cherry Creek HS and Aces Swim Club.

1. Mike Doherty.
Regis.

Note: Laurice "Lo" Hunter coached volleyball for 21 years at Evergreen High School. Her teams finished in the top five at the state championship 16 times, winning nine state titles. In seven seasons, her teams were undefeated. From 1978 to 1984, her teams won 182 consecutive games. What an amazing career by an amazing lady with unbelievable energy. She was recently inducted into the National High School Sports Hall of Fame. We asked Lo to name the top five athletes she coached at Evergreen from 1975 to 1995.

5. Courtney Putnam.
All-state volleyball, Texas Tech volleyball.

4. Paige Teel.
All-State Volleyball, Fort Lewis, all regionals.

3. Liz Armbrustmacher.
Colorado All-State, Indiana University starter for four years, Lakewood High School volleyball coach.

2. Sherri Danielson.
Colorado all-state volleyball, Colorado State University All-America honors, National USA Volleyball Team for four years, Olympic Team in Seoul, Korea.

1. Tanya Haave.
Colorado Sports Hall of Fame 1980 (Outstanding High School Athlete), Kodak All-American from University of Tennessee 1983, High School All-America 1980, University of San Francisco head basketball coach at this time.

Irv's 100 Best Ever High School Players in the Metro Area

If anyone in Denver is qualified to make a list like this, it's Irv. He has done some living.

100. Harry Narcisian, Wheat Ridge/CU.
They called him "The Horse" for a good reason: touch runner.

99. Steve Tracy, Lakewood/CU.
The only quarterback I have seen who was a nasty linebacker.

98. Dennis Rasmussen, Bear Creek/Creighton.
Basketball, baseball at both schools. Pitched 13 years in the Big Leagues.

97. Josh Bard, Cherry Creek.
Good catcher now with the San Diego Padres.

96. Barry Lensch, East.
A right-handed pitcher made it to the Bigs with Philly.

95. Tim Evans, Littleton/Stanford/CU.
Terrific shooter in basketball. After college signed a baseball contract with the Dodgers.

94. Dudley Mitchell, Thomas Jefferson/CU.
Played both basketball and baseball. Could really shoot. Played Double A ball in the Cardinal chain.

93. Don Sessions, Aurora Central/CU.
Solid quarterback and third baseman. Signed with Houston.

92. John Hesler, Brighton/CU.
A quarterback who had a great run in college. Continues to fight back after a bad auto accident.

91. Mark Mumford, Heritage/Nebraska.
Was a heck of a catcher and linebacker. Played for the Denver Broncos.

90. Steve Sidwell, East/CU.
Touch linebacker who had a lengthy career in the NFL as a defensive coordinator.

89. T.J. Cunningham, Overland/CU.
All-around skill in football.

88. Robin Burns, Arvada.
A terrific shortstop and quarterback.

87. Bob Bote, Littleton/CU.
Led the state in scoring in basketball. Led the state in touchdown passes. Played baseball at CU. One of the state's best prep coaches.

86. Gary Groninger, Green Mountain.
A terrific quarterback and catcher. Played at UNC then signed and played Minor League ball.

85. Rudy Carey, East.
You know he could coach. Did you know he's still in the record book at CSU for assists?

84. Herman Heard, South/Southern Colorado.
Had another gear. Played for the Kansas City Chiefs.

83. John Schmidt, Lutheran.
A good looking left-handed hitter; line drive guy.

82. Lavon Williams, Manual.
Great floor game. Went on to play at Kentucky.

81. Steve Blateric, Lincoln/DU.
Steady right-handed pitcher. Played with Cincinnati.

80. Pat Moriarty, East.
Single-wing tailback and a power hitter. Played at UNC. Signed with Cincinnati.

79. Dan Osborne, Westminster.
Hard thrower who made it to the Majors. Poppa Audie, a great hitter in softball.

78. Bill Stearns, Thomas Jefferson/Wyoming.
Football and baseball. Just a great tackler. Played baseball in college and signed with the Texas Rangers. Ended up a manager in AA.

77. Craig Bozich, Aurora Central/BYU.
A bruising linebacker.

76. Fred Tesone, Louisville/DU.
A quick halfback who was all-conference. Went on to become one of the best prep coaches in the state.

75. Joel Steed, Aurora Hinckley/CU.
Solid nose guard. Went on to play for the Steelers.

74. Ronnie Bradford, Adams City/CU.
A defensive back who played pro ball longer than teammates Deon Figures and Chris Hudson—both were Thorpe winners. Now a coach with the Broncos.

73. Carl Pigford, Manual/CSU.
Silky smooth.

72. Tom Rouen, Heritage/CU.
The punter who had good years with the Broncos.

71. Dennis Boone, Manual/Regis College.
The best jump-shooter we have ever had.

70. Harry Holliness, Manual.
Lefty was an All-American at DU.

69. Chuck Newcombe, East/CSU.
Had a great hook shot.

68. Hal Kinard, West/CSU.
The best defensive player to come out of the city.

67. Nick Wilhite, South.
First big bonus baby—got $50,000 from the Dodgers. Played with two teams in the Big Leagues.

66. Greg Jones, Kennedy/CU.
He was special in football and track. He played in the NFL with Washington.

65. Vincent White, Mullen/Stanford.
Had a great run, then played with the Denver Gold.

64. Craig Jackson, Montbello/UCLA.
The first big star at a new school. Great skills.

63. Bruce Vaughn, George Washington/UNC.
The best left-handed curve ball in the state.

62. Dan Antolini, Aurora Central/CU.
Best right-handed curve ball in the state.

61. Kay McFarland, Englewood.
Could do it all in football and track—same thing at CSU.

60. Fred Steinmark, Jr., Wheat Ridge/Texas.
One of the most beloved players ever in Austin. Died at the age of 22.

59. Art Unger, Manual.
Three-sport star. Same thing at CU. Just a great hitter when he played softball.

58. Taylor Tharp, Fairview.
The all-time leading passer in the state. Now the quarterback at Boise State.

57. Don Carlson, East.
Pitcher who made it to the Big Leagues with Pittsburgh.

56. Harvey Sterkel, North.
Back in the 50s he was a hard-throwing softball pitcher at City Park. He went on to be the best in the country with the Aurora Sealmaster out of Chicago.

55. Daniel Graham, Thomas Jefferson/CU.
Tight end first round pick to the Patriots. Got big money from the Broncos through free agency.

54. Mark Mullaney, George Washington/CSU.
Tough defensive lineman. Had a nice run with the Vikings.

53. Ron Herbel, Brighton.
Tough right-handed pitcher. Went to UNC. Signed and made it to the Giants.

52. Gary Schroeder, Westminster/CU. Basketball.
One of the most underrated players in this state.

51. Larry Farmer, Manual/UCLA.
Played with Lou Alcinder. Became the head coach at UCLA.

50. Mark Knudsen, Northglenn/CSU.
Right-handed pitcher, played several years in the Bigs. Beat Nolan Ryan on opening day. Used those infielders.

49. Kurt Wegener, Englewood.
Basketball and baseball. Hard-throwing pitcher. Made it to the Bigs with Philadelphia.

48. Devin Aguilar, Mullen.
Basketball and football. Always made the big play. Now at Washington.

47. Ben Brauch, Jefferson.
A dynamite infielder and basketball player who was solid at CU. Now plays Santa in the malls.

46. Terry Kunz, Wheat Ridge/CU.
A fullback who was tough as they made them. Played in the NFL with the Oakland Raiders.

45. Marcus Houston, Thomas Jefferson.
The number-one recruit his senior year. Played at CU and CSU.

44. Lendale White, Chatfield.
Bruising running back who played on a national championship team at USC. First round pick at Tennessee. The best is ahead.

43. Tyler Green, Thomas Jefferson/Wichita State.
A pitcher with a knuckle curve as good as Burt Hooton. Played several years with the Phillies.

42. Mike Schnitker, Lakewood.
Transferred from George Washington. All-state end, played at CU and moved to guard. Played several years for the Broncos.

41. Bill Garnett, Regis/Wyoming.
The fourth pick overall in the NBA Draft by Dallas.

40. Dean Lahr, North.
The best wrestler ever from the state. Two-time NCAA champ out of CU, and the MVP in the Olympic trials.

39. Rick Fisher, George Washington.
Three-sport athlete. Tremendous skills. Went on to star in basketball at CSU.

38. Kevin McDougal, Arvada West/CSU.
All-conference both places. I liked him at safety.

37. Brad Pyatt, Arvada West/Kentucky/UNC.
Can fly. Was the Indianapolis return man until he got hurt. Now plays Arena Football.

36. Stevie Johnson, Manual.
Yes, he was the middleweight champion of the world at one time. But he was a super quick tailback that Purdue offered a full ride.

35. Kelli McGregor, Lakewood. Big tight end.
Was an All-American at CSU. Played with the Denver Broncos.

34. Pat Frink, Wheat Ridge/CU.
Maybe the best pure shooter ever. Played with the Big "O" at Cincinnati.

33. John Karramigios, West.
The Galloping Greek from Cherry Creek (named by Manual Boody). All-city running back at West. All-conference at DU.

32. Mark Randall, Cherry Creek.
Ultimate team player. Went to Kansas. Look it up—he went head-to-head with Shaq. First round pick of the Bulls.

31. Jay Howell, Fairview.
Pitcher drafted out of high school. Went to CU then signed after junior year. Had a great run with several clubs as a reliever.

30. Scott Wedman, Mullen.
Strong, great shooter. All-conference at CU. First round pick Kansas City Kings.

29. Matt Bouldin, Thunder Ridge.
A big 6-foot-5 point guard. The best prospect the state has had in years. He's at Gonzaga.

28. Jim Deidel, Mullen.
Three-sport athlete. Played in the Yankee chain and got to the Big Leagues. The problem was he was a catcher and the pin stripes had Thurman Munson.

27. Chris Babbs, East.
Four-sport star. Baseball in the summer. Won all three sprints at the state track meet.

26. Stan Williams, East.
Basketball and baseball. Played with the LA Dodgers, won 106 games. Same staff as Don Drysdale, Sandy Koufax and Johnny Podres. Now a scout.

25. Lee Kunz, Wheat Ridge.
All-state fullback. Won the state high jump and pole vault and he weighed 220 pounds.

24. Chuck Williams, East.
Three-sport athlete. Played basketball at CU, then played in the NBA.

23. Richard Tate, East.
All-around athlete. Played basketball at Utah.

22. Art Bunte, South.
Built like a tank, could rebound, soft touch. An All-American at Utah.

21. Joe Romig, Lakewood.
Probably should be ranked higher. All-American halfback in high school. That's when tear-aways started. All-American at CU as a lineman.

20. Ken Charlton, South/CU.
All-American basketball player. Could shoot and rebound despite bad knees.

19. Joe Strain, George Washington.
Three-sport star. Played baseball at UNC. A couple of years with the Giants. He's a scout for San Francisco.

18. Bill Faddis, Regis.
Three-sport star and the best infielder ever to come out of the state. Played at USC.

17. Bruno Konopka, Manual.
Still holds the nation's record for a 99-yard punt. Bruno was a power hitting first baseman. He played for Connie Mack and the Philadelphia A's.

16. Danny Jackson, Aurora Central.
This left-handed pitcher was a star with Cincinnati and the Kansas City Royals. Won 22 games with the latter.

15. Tony Boselli, Fairview/USC.
When he was in the NFL before tearing up a shoulder, he was considered the best tackle in the game.

14. Eloy, Annunciation.
All-state in three sports. Played football at Trinidad and DU. Went back to coach Annunciation.

13. Ron Shavlick, East.
All-American at North Carolina State. Held all the scoring and rebounding records for years in the ACC. Drafted in the first round by the Knicks.

12. Chuck Darling, South.
Big guy, All-American at Iowa. Played in the Olympics.

11. Tom Chambers, Fairview.
Was an All-American with Utah and an all-pro with Phoenix in the NBA. Selected as the MVP in the All-Star game.

10. Roy Halladay, Arvada West.
Dominant guy who got even better in pro ball. Won the Cy Young with Toronto.

9. Steve Zabel, Thornton.
Three-sport athlete was an all-conference linebacker at OU, and an all-pro with New England. Threw the baseball 90 mph.

8. Bobby Anderson, Boulder/CU.
All-American running back who was a quarterback until his senior year. Drafted in the first round by the Broncos. He could have signed in baseball—switch hitting catcher.

7. Chauncey Billups, George Washington.
All-American basketball player at CU. First round draft pick in the NBA. Nuggets had him for a while; should have kept him. He's the Piston's MVP.

6. Darnell McDonald, Cherry Creek.
The best running back ever to come out of here. Had a full ride at Texas. Went the pro baseball route. Is with the Orioles chain in AAA.

5. Dick Anderson, Boulder.
Star football player, all-league at CU and all-pro with Miami. Is a consistent winner on the amateur golf tour.

4. Amy Van Dyken, Cherry Creek/CSU.
Star swimmer in the Olympics. *Sports Illustrated* picked her number three in the 50 greatest sports figures of the 20th century from Colorado, listed just after Jack Dempsey and Whizzer White.

3. John Stearns, Thomas Jefferson.
Three-sport star played baseball and football at CU. All-conference in both. Drafted number two by Major League Baseball. Played 10 years with the Mets; was an all-star.

2. Hale Irwin, Boulder.

A star football player. All-conference safety at CU. One of the best golfers ever on the PGA Tour.

1. Dave Logan, Wheat Ridge.

The only guy in our state drafted in all three sports. An All-American end at CU. Played for years with the Cleveland Browns.

Things You Might Not Know About Irv :: Joe Williams

What new or surprising fact can I say about a man who talks on the air for four hours a day? Irv Brown is a fossilized relic of everything great about Denver sports. He's a hometown hero, a proud grad of North High. Some of our callers call him Coach. He was a coach, of course. But it's also in honor of his ongoing contributions to developing local sports talent. Here are a few things that you might not know about Irv.

9. He's a Hall of Famer many times over.
He has been inducted into the Colorado High School Hall of Fame, the University of Northern Colorado Hall of Fame and the Colorado Sports Hall of Fame.

8. He's a Denver Nuggets Community Ambassador.
7. He coached for 25 years.
At the high school level and at Metro State College and the University of Colorado.

6. He's had a 25-year career as a college basketball referee, including 6 Final Fours.
He also supervised basketball officials in the Western Athletic Conference, Big Sky and Midwestern cities conference.

5. He's had a long career as a broadcaster.
He has worked for CBS, ESPN, Prime Sports Network, Raycom and Blue White Network. He has been a talk show host, a Denver Nuggets analyst and even had a weekly cable TV show.

4. He's a motivational speaker.
He's done presentations for companies and organizations such as Wells Fargo, State Farm, Blue Cross and the University of Illinois Quarterback Club.

3. He was a professional baseball scout.
For the Houston Astros, Kansas City Royals and Philadelphia Phillies.

2. He's on *Sports Illustrated*'s list.
When the magazine was selecting the top 50 Colorado sports figures of the 20th Century, Irv made the list at number 39.

1. He's the founder of Colorado's Gold C Book.
I probably still have one of these discount-coupon books from 25 years ago in a drawer somewhere. You probably do, too.

Irv was a college basketball official for 25 years in nine different leagues. He worked six Final Fours. Here are his five most memorable.

5. 1982.

This was Irv's last game, in Cedar Rapids, Iowa. The ACC All-Stars vs. the Big Ten. The opposing coaches were Al McGuire and Billy Packer. Doing the TV was Dick Enberg and Bob Knight.

4. 1976.

Indiana beat Michigan to cap an unbeaten season for Bob Knight. Knight is a frequent caller on our show. He loves to kid Irv about this game. The Hoosiers had an undefeated team. All five starters were first round picks in the NBA including the MVP Scott May. Irv and Bob Wortman were the officials. In the very first minute of play, Bobby Wilkerson was knocked unconscious on the baseline. Neither Wortman nor Irv saw what happened. The trainer snapped an amcap under Wilkerson's nose, but Bobby never moved. NBC was televising the game. They went to a commercial break. During the time out, Knight gave it to Irv the whole time as they prepared to take Wilkerson to the hospital. Knight had a classic remark as he returned to the bench, "Brown, on the back of your driver's license there's a section on what to do with your organs. When you die, give your eyes to the blind. You've never used them."

3. 1973.

At the Astrodome UCLA beats Villanova for the National Championship. Villanova featured Howard Porter, the tournament MVP. He had signed early with an agent and Villanova had to give the money back.

2. 1972.

Florida State beats Kentucky. Adolph Rupp's last game.

1. 1969.

NCAA Final Purdue vs. UCLA. Lew Alcindor's (Kareem Abdul-Jabbar's) last game in college. John Wooden wins another one.

Explosive Basketball Coaches

Here are the coaches who really got after Irv when he was a referee. All have been guests on our talk show.

4. Bob Knight.

The winningest men's basketball coach of all time, at Army, Indiana and currently at Texas Tech. He would test you. Remember the chair throw? He got the Big Ten officials a pay raise.

3. Don Haskins.

UTEP. Hall of Famer. Subject of the movie *Glory Road*. He was a great competitor on the bench. Don had a great assistant, Gene Iba. Many times, Haskins would pick up three technical fouls, get ejected and Iba would do a superb job. When Haskins is a guest on our radio show, the subject of the 1966 NCAA Championship always comes up. Haskins made history by starting five African American players for the first time in a championship game. They faced Kentucky's all-white squad, coached by Adolph Rupp. Haskins also talks about a guy named Herman Carr, a retired mail carrier living in Denver. The two grew up together in Oklahoma and played hours of one-on-one basketball.

2. Al McGuire.

Marquette University's men's basketball coach from 1964 to 1977. As much fun as any coach ever. He went to the NIT and won it. At a regional tournament he put an official on his all-opponent team.

1.Jim Williams.

CSU. Coached 25 seasons. The winingest coach in Colorado history. He picked up six technical fouls vs. Tulsa. When the game was over, it was over. He never held a grudge.

Irv's Secrets for Success in Sports :: Irv Brown

I was a seven-letter athlete at North High School and have coached, officiated and commented on sports my whole career. I officiated six NCAA Final Four championship games, which were big highlights for me. But coaching was my favorite gig. I coached a lot of great young people. Some players went on to professional careers—guys like Jay Howell, MLB relief pitcher who was a member of the LA Dodgers when they won the World Series in 1988. I also coached John Stearns, outstanding catcher for the NY Mets. When Stearns was 17 years old he was drafted by the Oakland Athletics but opted to go to school at the University of Colorado instead. Sometimes people ask me for advice. That just shows you how misguided they are to begin with. I'm no guru, but here are few things I've learned.

5. You have to be willing to make the tough calls, the unpopular calls that make the fans boo and the coaches yell.

To work the big games, you have to have to be assertive, send strong signals and call it the way you see it. You'll develop a reputation for fairness and integrity. Then, even when you make a bad call—and I've made some memorable bad calls—you won't lose the trust of players and coaches.

4. To excel in sports, you have to be a competitor.

You have to devote time to conditioning and practice. You might have tremendous natural ability, but to develop your talent you have to put in the time. If you don't have a lot of natural talent, you can learn solid fundamentals and become tougher, smarter and better conditioned. You might not become a star, but you can become better than average. Talent or no, you're only as good as your attitude and how hard you're willing to work.

3. You're gonna get knocked down.

You gotta get back up again. If you just stay down and feel sorry for yourself, you're gonna lose. Learn how to put mistakes and bad performances behind you quickly. No one likes to lose but you can't win every time.

2. In any profession, the people who win are the ones with guts and personality.

Your personality is whatever it is—quiet, serious, outgoing, friendly, mischievous, whatever. It doesn't matter so much WHAT your personality is. It's just important that you have one. People can get to know you and relate to you through your personality.

1. Chemistry and rapport are everything.

The way to get a rapport going is to communicate. Talk to people. Learn people's names. Get to know them and let them get to know you. Develop relationships. This is fairly easy for me because I like to talk to people. Granted, not everyone is going to like you, and you're not going to like everyone either. Still, communication—with teammates, coaches, officials, players, co-workers, etcetera—is indispensable for success.

Zebras from Denver

Denver has produced eleven NFL officials.

11. Alabama Glass.
Worked 15 years. One Super Bowl. Was a star player at CU.

10. Pete Liske.
Eight years. One Super Bowl. He was a solid quarterback at Penn State and in the CFL.

9. Ron Liebsack.
Five years.

8. Ben Dreith.
30 years. Two Super Bowls. A three-sport athlete at UNC.

7. Kent Payne.
Four years. Still working. He's a teacher.

6. Jim Saracino.
13 years. One Super Bowl. He's a teacher.

5. Bill Schmitz.
10 years. One Super Bowl. Played at CSU.

4. Howard Roe.
12 years. Wore the white hat.

3. Bob Frederic.
20 years. Classy guy who was tough. Played football at CU.

2. Pat Haggerty.
20 years. Three Super Bowls.

1. Tom Fincken.
24 years. Three Super Bowls. Retired teacher.

Notable Broncos Assistants

These one-time Broncos assistant coaches were also head coaches in either college or the pros.

10. Kay Daulton.
Did a great job at the University of Northern Colorado. Great teacher of quarterbacks.

9. Paul Roach.
Wyoming. He won the tough WAC two straight years.

8. Greg Robinson.
5 years. Syracuse. He was the Broncos defensive coordinator in two Super Bowls.

7. Ray Rhodes.
2 years. Philadelphia, Green Bay.

6. Wade Phillips.
4 years. Buffalo, Dallas. Won 13 games.

5. Gary Kubiak.
11 years. Houston Texans. He's got them on the move.

4. Chan Gailey.
4 years. Dallas Cowboys. Back in the league as offensive coordinator at Kansas City.

3. Jim Fassel.
1993-1994. New York Giants. He got to the Super Bowl.

2. Joe Collier.
1972-1981. Buffalo Bills. Great defensive mind.

1. Raymond Berry.
1991. New England Patriots. We love his patience.

Local Team Nicknames

Here are our five favorite team nicknames.

5. The Little Monsters.

The DU football team. In the late forties, they had a good club with a very small line. In those days they were very productive. Nobody weighed more than 180. The center was Joe Cribari. The guards were Dick Yates and Bob Webber. The tackles were Steve Woytek and Gene Beauchamp. The ends were Greg Browning and Mike Peterson. A fun group. DU played football until the mid-sixties.

4. Rocktober 2007.

Refers to the 2007 Colorado Rockies and the greatest run we've ever seen. When the Rox got a two-out, ninth-inning homerun from Todd Helton off previously unhitable Ted Saito, it began the greatest run in baseball history. The club won 21 of 22. On September 16th they were four-and-one-half games back from the Wild Card with a slew of teams ahead of them. Since entering the league in 1993, Colorado had never won more than 83 games. In 2007, they won 90 and they did it with pitching. They had a league best 2.08 ERA in their seven playoff games.

3. Buzz Boys.

Regis College basketball in the late forties captured a crowd of fans around here. They won 30-plus games. Larry Varnell had a great, cohesive team. Bobby Wallace and Dick Petry were the guards. Bryce Hefley was in the middle. The forwards were Harvey Moore and Bob Fisher.

2. Blake Street Bombers.

General Manager Bob Gebhardt put together a group of power hitters that brought flocks of fans to the ballpark. Ellis Burks, Larry Walker, Andres Galarraga, Dante Bichette and Vinny Castilla. This was before the humidor and they just killed the ball. They had power on the road, too. Galarraga hit a ball off Kevin Brown that traveled 629 feet. Larry Walker holds the record at Coors Field. He hit one 493 feet against Oakland.

1. Orange Crush.

A soda pop distributor came up with this for the Broncos defense the first time they went to the Super Bowl. Joe Collier was a great coordinator. He played a three-four that featured Lyle Alzado, Tom Jackson, Randy Gradishar and Billy Thompson. Great team speed.

Great Names and Nicknames in Colorado Sports

Here's a list of names and nicknames we like to say.

Moose Womack.
First base. Denver Bears.

Tippy Martinez.
CSU Baseball.

Choo Freeman.
Former Rockies outfielder. Caught more touchdown passes (50) than any player in Texas prep history.

Virgil Jester.
Pitcher in American Legion A baseball every Sunday afternoon at the old Elitches, long ago.

Rudolfo "Corky" Gonzales.
Great fighter in the forties.

Mildred "Babe" Didrikson Zaharias.
Maybe the best female athlete ever.

Rich "Goose" Gossage.
MLB Hall of Fame.

Joe "Awful" Coffee.
Colorado Hall of Fame Boxer.

Thurman "Fum" McGraw.
Detroit Lions great.

Robert "Ace" Gruenig.
Early Nuggets.

Frankie Sinkwich.
Amateur football during WW II at DU Stadium.

Elroy "Crazy Legs" Hirsch.
Amateur football during WW II at DU Stadium.

Earl "Dutch" Clark.
Pro football.

"The Mannasa Mauler."
Jack Dempsey.

Byron "Whizzer" White.
Chief Justice. Never liked the nickname.

John "Hatchet Man" Wooten.
CU football.

Dan "The Horse" Issel.
Played and coached the Denver Nuggets

Allan "The Horse" Hower.
Played at Regis College and coached Mapleton High School.

Harry "The Horse" Narcisian.
Played at CU and coached at Wheat Ridge.

Boyd "Tiny" Grant.
Competed in both basketball and baseball at CSU. Then became the head basketball coach. Sox Walseth did the same thing at CU.

Russell "Sox" Walseth.
CU men's hoops coach. They named the court after him.

Forrest "Frosty" Cox.
Played basketball at KU then coached CU to three conference titles and five finals from 1935 to 1950.

Sportscasters We'll Never Forget

We've listened to and met a lot of great local sportscasters over the years. As sports radio guys, we know it's not easy to make sportscasting sound like it's easy. Here's a shout out to some of the most memorable voices and faces of Colorado sports, past and present. In no particular order.

Larry Varnell.
He was one of the very first in the 1950s. The Regis College basketball coach would stand up with no notes and no teleprompter and deliver sports.

Brian Drees.
No one worked harder to fit pictures with the story. Great genes. His father Jack was a legend in Chicago.

Starr Yelland.
He and Channel 7 news owned the ratings.

Mike Nolan.
Smooth delivery. Formed a great play-by-play team with Ben Martin doing Air Force football games.

Kevin Corke.
Funny, energetic. Left to go to ESPN. Now ABC.

Gary Cruz.
Huge following. "Gary Cruz, Nine News." Got a little bit carried away doing Broncos games in pre-season.

Dan Ryan.
Had a rough time here. He did a feature about sky diving when he first got here and did the show for weeks from a hospital bed. Had a classic boo-boo doing the Bill Mallory show and forgot who CU had played.

Lynn Sanner.
Great guy who passed away way too soon after he moved here from Salt Lake City.

Bob Kurtz.
Had a rough time saying his name. Lots of turnovers on his segment.

Mike Hafner.
Former Bronco did the first Denver Rockets televised games.

Steve Alvarez.
Pretty good weekend guy.

Les Shapiro.

Ratings were good. A lot of people wonder why he hasn't hooked on again.

David Treadwell.

Former Broncos kicker was Fox's first sports anchor. We thought there was potential, but he didn't stay long in the gig.

Steve Harms.

CBS local sports anchor. Survived a throat operation to have a nice run. He had a solid talk show with Sandy Clough on KYBG. Now in Salt Lake City broadcasting minor league hockey.

Ron Zapollo.

He was the best. All the teams trusted him and gave him inside information. You had to watch him every night. Now does the news on Fox.

Tom Green.

Another guy who has gone over to the news side. The greatest sense of humor and terrific timing.

Tom Green is one of the most popular media figures in Denver. His early days were at ESPN as a sports anchor. He came to Denver in the 80s as a sports anchor and had a great run. Then did a talk show with Doug Moe on KKFN, the station Irv and Joe are on. He currently anchors the Emmy-award winning News2 This Morning on WGN-TV in the morning. Several years ago he had a popular trivia show on ESPN called "Sports On Tap." Tom lists his top five trivia shows.

5. The Joker's Wild.
"Where knowledge is king and lady luck is queen." Perfectly mindless.

4. Sports Challenge.
A 1970s classic. Worth watching if only to see Dick Enberg's jackets. In the Bonus Biography round, players had 60 seconds to identify an athlete, pictured in silhouette, based on clues.

3. Password.
Hosted by Allen Ludden. He won a Daytime Emmy for it in 1976. One of the first shows to have a Lightning Round. Love the classics.

2. Jeopardy.
Maybe the only intelligent game show ever.

1. Sports On Tap.
Did you expect anything different? A decent sports trivia game show that was brilliantly hosted.

A Dozen Great Interviews :: Mark McIntosh

Note: Mark McIntosh was an all-around athlete with a football scholarship to Missouri. He was projected to be a Major League Baseball first-round pick. He suffered a fractured skull in a basketball game, and that ended his athletic career. You might remember him from CBS4 News in Denver. Mark has had a 20-year career in television broadcasting and does a lot of community service work. He and Denise Plante are co-hosts of the "Colorado and Company" show. Mark lists the top 12 sports celebrities he has covered as a broadcaster.

12. Larry Walker.
Pure talent.

11. Matt Holliday.
Hall of Fame potential.

10. Troy Tulowitzski.
Fearless.

9. Todd Helton.
Mr. Consistent.

8. LaPhonso Ellis.
Great talent and desire.

7. Terrell Davis.
Overachiever.

6. Champ Bailey.
The best athlete.

5. Steve Atwater.
Big hitter.

4. Alfred Williams.
An animal off the edge.

3. Mike Pritchard.
Tough to tackle.

2. Darian Hagan.
Mr. Magic.

1. John Elway.
Accessible and simply the best.

Golden Voices :: Jim Conrad

Note: Jim Conrad was the Sports Director at KWGN-TV in Denver for 22 years. What a voice this guy has. He has been doing play-by-play, broadcasting and voice overs for 30 years. A real talent. We asked him to list the top five best-ever local sportscasters.

5. Lynn Sanner.
One of the all-time nice guys and well respected by everyone.

4. Larry Zimmer.
Very versatile sportscaster, very knowledgeable and has excellent rapport with athletes, coaches and owners.

3. Ron Zappolo.
Knows how to use TV and his position to influence. Very well respected by athletes and coaches. Very versatile.

2. Starr Yelland.
Ultimate showman, knew how to use his position to bring attention to people and sports he wanted to promote, extremely popular with viewers and athletes.

1. Bob Martin.
Consummate professional, perhaps the smartest man I've ever known. Could handle any situation and had complete knowledge of almost every sport. (Also, gave me my first job in TV!!!)

Favorite Soccer Moments :: Vic Lombardi

Note: Vic Lombardi, the 19-time Emmy Award winner and sports anchor on CBS4, was born and raised on Denver's North Side. He went Holy Family High School and CU Boulder. He played soccer and is a big supporter of the sport. Here are Vic's top five soccer moments:

5. I score my first goal as a High School freshman at Holy Family.
We end up losing to Summit County by the slim margin of 12-1.

4. Colorado awarded MLS team in 1995.
Marcelo Balboa named captain.

3. 2006, Marco Matterazzi head butted by Zinedine Zidane.
Italy wins the cup.

2. 2004, U.S. advances to semi-finals of the World Cup in Japan.
1. 1982, Italy wins the World Cup in Mexico City.
We drove our cars through the streets of North Denver in celebration.

An Anchor Picks His Top News Stories :: Jim Benemann

Note: Emmy-award winning journalist Jim Benemann anchors the news at CBS 4. Jim lists five of the biggest local news stories in no particular order, putting a major sports story in weighty company.

The Pope Visits Colorado, 1993.
There was so much anticipation for the Pope's arrival and he didn't disappoint. John Paul had tremendous charisma and tremendous affection for young Catholics. The young pilgrims who came to Colorado for his visit and World Youth Day fed off of that. Cherry Creek State Park was packed for the Papal Mass. The Pope also visited Regis University and met President Clinton there. That was another remarkable moment as I was there reporting on the event.

Columbine High School Shootings, 1999.
A day that will, of course, live in infamy in Colorado. I was at home when my wife asked if I'd heard the news. At first all we knew was that there was at least one gunman in the high school. By the time police entered the school it was all over. As we learned more about the beautiful young people who were massacred we were also learning about the twisted hatred that led two of their classmates to kill them and wound others. A genuine tragedy.

Broncos Win their First Super Bowl, 1998.
John Elway and his mates were 9-point underdogs going in against the feared Packers. But it was Green Bay that looked outclassed as the Broncos proved to be the more physical and determined team. The game included the now famous play with Elway getting spun around like a top as he fought for a first down. It was great to see the Hall of Fame QB win the title he so richly deserved.

Hayman Wildfire, 2002.
It was the year of the drought and when that fire took off it became an inferno that burned up 16 square miles. It was the largest wildfire in Colorado history. The plot thickened when we learned a Forest Service employee sparked the fire thinking she could quickly put it out and become a hero. It will take generations for the scorched lands southwest of Denver to recover.

Timothy McVeigh Bombing Trial, 1997.
A heartless killer is found guilty in Denver on all counts in connection with the bombing two years earlier of the Murrah Federal building in Oklahoma City. 168 people, including 19 children died when the building exploded. McVeigh showed no remorse during the trial. I was in Terre Haute, Indiana when McVeigh was executed. No one was sorry to see him go.

These are guys who have played pro ball in Denver, and who have done a regular shift on sports talk radio. In no particular order.

Dave Logan.

After a long career in the NFL he has been doing talk radio about twenty years, starting out at KLAK, now a fixture at KOA.

Jim Ryan.

Denver Broncos linebacker for ten years, now a Broncos coach. Did a regular shift on three different stations.

Scott Hastings.

NBA veteran who was a NBA Champion with Detroit. He wound up his career with the Denver Nuggets. Started out at KOA and now has a regular shift with former Bronco Alfred Williams on KKFN. Alfred was a starter on a Super Bowl Champion team.

Jim Turner and Mike Haffner.

They have a solid talk show on KNUS. Turner had a great run with the Jets and Broncos, and is in the Ring of Fame. Haffner, a single wing tailback at UCLA was a wide receiver for the Broncos.

Mark Knudsen.

Veteran Major League pitcher who once beat Nolan Ryan on opening day. Wound up his career with the Rockies. Did a regular shift on KKFN with Jim Tatum who played for the Rockies.

Tom Glassic.

A number-one pick for the Broncos, he had a brief run with Jay Mariotti on KNUS.

Dan Issel.

Denver Nuggets player and coach in the Hall of Fame. Did a shift with Tom Green and Sandy Clough on KKFN.

Doug Moe.

Head Coach of the Nuggets and now an assistant coach there. He had a regular shift with Tom Green on KKFN.

Note: Bob Martin did the greatest voice play-by-play for the Broncos. He stood the whole game. Never used a chart, just worked off a program. He lists some of the big names in local sports media, in no particular order. If you're an old-timer, you ought to remember these guys.

Harry Farrar.
Created the fictitious character named Sam Pirkle. His English was superb.

Fred Leo.
He was at Channel 2. Did a lot of Bears and Zephyrs games on TV.

Bill Reed.
He was the play-by-play announcer for the Denver Bears. He would recreate the games on the road. Great voice, classy dresser. He would take his pants off during the game so he wouldn't lose the crease.

Leonard Catin.
Rocky Mountain News columnist. Loved the AAU Tourney.

Chet Nelson.
Rocky Mountain News sports editor.

Jack Carberry.
Denver Post sports editor. Started the Post Parokes All-Star Game.

Starr Yelland.
In the 70s, Starr, Bob Palmer, and Warren Chandler at Channel 7 owned the market.Dick Connor. *Denver Post* Columnist. He's so popular he has a street named after him.

Frank Haraway.
He and June never missed a baseball game. The *Post* columnist also was the official scorekeeper for the Bears and Rockies.

Players Who Made Me an Avalanche Fan
:: Aaron D'Albey

Note: In late 2007 Aaron compiled years of hockey-related, angst-fueled Internet banter and created *The Dog and Pony Show*, "hockey reading for the mildly concussed," a hockey blog dedicated to finding the fun in everything hockey. Check it out at http://thednp.blogspot.com/. Here are Aaron's top ten Avs.

10. Mike Ricci.

This virile god of all things rink spent just over two years with the Avs in Denver while receiving constant abuse about the head and neck. Yet if there is a man who can attract more women while sporting no teeth and a mullet, I haven't met him.

9. Claude Lemieux.

Every good story needs a villain, and every champion needs a skilled and calculating pest. Few players could make an opposing team bristle quite like Claude could, and without Claude I doubt the Avalanche would have met with as much success as they did.

8. Uwe Krupp.

I like Uwe. Not just because I was one of about 17 fans who were still awake when he finally won the Avs their first Stanley Cup with a wicked slapper from the right point. But because he only played 30 games over the next four seasons for the Red Wings due to back problems, potting all of 6 points during that time. Way to give 'em nothing, Uwe!

7. Shjon Podein.

Podein's greatest accomplishment isn't that he created The Shjon Podein Children's Foundation, but that he remained dressed in his pads for twenty-five hours after winning the Cup in 2001. Now THAT is HOCKEY!

6. Bob Hartley.

Okay I threw in a coach. But really, if the CIA needs to train people to spy on Canada, then have them listen to tapes of Bob's post-game interviews. He is the reason I can now speak Canadian.

5. Chris Drury.

Nicknamed "Clutch" because of his ability to always be in the right place at the right time, Drury is known to many Avs fans as the kid credited with winning the Little League World Series, helping the Avalanche to a Stanley Cup victory before being wrongly traded to Calgary, and saving Earth from Martian attack on numerous occasions.

4. Paul Stastny.

He plays with an old wooden stick in old, beaten up hockey skates, and comes from one of the great families in the sport. The puck follows him around like a puppy, and he came to the NHL from DU already missing teeth. His name is Paul, and he is here to win a Stanley Cup.

3. Patrick Roy.

Simply, he was the greatest goaltender in history. It is all about respect. No goalie instilled the kind of respect in shooters that St. Patrick did, and few ever will. If you have any questions, his ears are plugged with Stanley Cup rings and he can't hear you.

2. Peter Forsberg.

What other player would prompt this kind of fevered telephone conversation: "So you're telling me he's playing tonight. Who told you that? You read it where? He's what? He's in Sweden again?! No? So he's in Denver. He has to play! Okay, so he's playing tonight? Who told you that? You read it where?! . . . ."

1. Joe Sakic.

The best wrist shot ever. The epitome of leadership. Completely dry in an interview. Pick the line that isn't a "Quoteless Joe" classic:

- "I thought we played really hard tonight."

- "I thought the other team played really hard tonight."

- "Are those . . . Bugle Boy Jeans you're wearing?"

Useless but interesting tidbits of knowledge to feed your hungry sports brain:

15. George Boedecker.
The founder of world-famous Crocs footwear was a point guard at Fairview High School.

14. Mike Landis.
The veteran news anchor was a sprinter in high school. He ran the hundred in 9.9.

13. Troy Tulowitzki.
The Rockies shortstop was 15 and 1 on the mound his junior year in high school, and he averaged 22 points a game his senior year in basketball.

12. Todd Helton.
The Rockies veteran along with Lou Gehrig, Albert Pujols, Babe Ruth and Ted Williams are the only five players in major league history to possess a .330 batting average, .400 on-base percentage and .600 slugging percentage in their careers.

11. Ryne Duren.
The MLB pitcher made his debut with the Denver Bears in the second game of a double-header at Bears Stadium. The opponent was Wichita. Duren threw his first warm-up pitch halfway up the backstop. Irv is convinced he did it on purpose. By the way, he threw a no-hitter.

10. Purple Row.
The 20th row of upper deck seats at Coors Field marks one-mile elevation above sea level.

9. John Stearns.
The soon-to-be MLB catcher had the play of the football game when CU won the 1971 Astro Blue Bonnet Bowl. Back to punt on his own nine yard line, there was no rush. Stearns ran for a first down to let the Buffs go on and win.

8. Larry Walker.
The former Rockies slugger belted eight of the 26 upper-deck homeruns at Coors Field.

7. Bobby Riggs.
The tennis hustler beat Bobby Anderson 6-2 in a charity tennis match in 1975 while wearing Anderson's Denver Broncos uniform—helmet and shoulder pads included—and an ankle weight for good measure.

6. Bill Ritter.
Colorado's Governor was the captain of Gateway's football team.

5. Larry Varnell.
The Denver Nugget coached Stan Musial during World War II.

4. Susie Wargin.
The sports anchor on Channel 9 was team manager for several sports at Broomfield High School.

3. Sinbad.
The comedian played basketball at DU. His real name is David Adkins.

2. Dinger.
The Colorado Rockies dinosaur mascot was chosen because workers found several dinosaur fossils in the ground during construction of Coors Field.

1. James Naismith.
The inventor of the game of basketball lived in Denver and was the first physical director of the Central Denver YMCA in the 1800s when he was a medical student at what was to become the University of Colorado.

Hoop Dreams at the Auditorium Arena

Here's a blast from the past. Before the NBA, there was the ABA. Before the ABA, there were the Amateur Athletic Union and the "elite" teams of the National Basketball League (NBL.) Good times. We used to watch basketball at the Auditorium Arena. That probably means nothing to you. The Auditorium Arena, which used to be at 13th and Champa, ain't what it used to be. It's all dressed up now as the Ellie Caulkins Opera House or the Buell Theatre or something. In 1935, right in the heart of the Great Depression, the AAU tournament moved to Denver from Kansas City. Don't dismiss this as an insignificant moment in Denver sports. This was a big deal. It was the biggest sporting event in Denver at the time. It put our town on the national sports map. Some of the great players we watched: Leonard Alterman, Vince Boryla, Gary Thompson, Rick Barry, Frank Lubin, Jim Pollard and Kenny Sailors. The tournament lasted until 1968 when we got an ABA team. Here are some of the more memorable names and teams from wayback. Team names had a lot to do with corporate sponsorship.

Peoria Cats.
Wichita Vickers.
Akron Goodyears.
Coached by Hank Vaughn. Also, Akron Wingfoots. Another team was the Akron Firestone Non-Skids.

Denver Safeway Stores.
Called "the Safeways." Previously, they were the Denver Piggly Wigglys. Fans called them the Pigs. I'm not making this up.

Denver American Legion.
Denver Ambrose-Legion.
Denver Murphy Mahoney.
Denver Chevrolets.
Or Denver Chevvies.

Denver Capital.
Denver Central Bankers.
Denver Ambrose Jellymakers.
Jellymakers can be fierce.

Denver Nuggets.
With Ace Gruenig and Jumpin' Jack McCracken.

Phillips 66ers.
From Oklahoma. They were always the favorite and won many titles. They were always the "villain" for locals to root against, with the likes of Shorty Carpenter, Bob Kurland and Cab Renick.

Luckett-Nix Clippers.

From Boulder. They went to the finals in the 1955, losing to Phillips66ers by the ominous score of 66 to 64. Birdie Haldorson, Bob Jeangerard, Charlie Mock, Tom Harrold and Bob Yardley played. The coach was a CU football player Freddy Johnson.

Poudre Valley Creamery.

From Fort Collins. In 1951, they went to the finals, losing to Stewart Chevrolet from San Francisco, coached by Hank Luisetti. Poudre Valley was a collection of Colorado A&M players: Bill Gosset, George Janzen, Glendon Anderson and Johnny O'Boyle.

Top Basketball Players from Back in the Day
:: Vince Boryla

Note: Vince Boryla was an All-American basketball star at Notre Dame and the University of Denver. Folks called him "Moose." Vince represented our country in the Olympics as a member of the team that won gold in London in 1948. He played for the New York Knickerbockers from 1949 to 1954. Vince averaged 12 points a game. He later coached the Knicks, from 1956 to 1958, and was general manager from 1958 to 1964. He came back to Denver to serve as GM for the Nuggets. We asked Vince to name the top 5 players he played against.

5. Arnie Johnson.
Strong. Great rebounder.

4. Bill Sharman.
Tenacious. A better-than-average defender.

3. Bobby Davies.
Quick. A very good shooter.

2. Jim Pollard.
Could run. A great leaper.

1. George Mikan.
Built like a tank. Could run. Could hook with both hands.

Note: Ceal Barry, popular coach of University of Colorado women's basketball, retired from coaching after the 2004–05 season. She coached the Buffs for 22 seasons, retiring with an impressive all-time record of 510-284 and .642 winning percentage. She's a member of the Colorado Sports Hall of Fame. We asked her to list the top 10 women who played basketball in Colorado.

10. Erin Scholz.
Doherty High School, University of Colorado 1993-1997.

9. Mandy Nightingale.
Sapulpa High School, University of Colorado 1999-2003.

8. Abby Waner.
Thunder Ridge High School, Duke University.

7. Becky Hammon.
South Dakota, Colorado State University mid 1990s.

6. Jamillah Lang.
Kansas City, University of Colorado 1990-1994.

5. Jamie Carey.
Horizon High School, Stanford University, University of Texas.

4. Ann Strother.
Highlands Ranch High School, University of Connecticut.

3. Tanya Haave.
Evergreen High School, University of Tennessee.

2. Shelley Sheetz.
Cedar Rapids Iowa, Kennedy High School, University of Colorado 1991-1995.

1. Bridget Turner.
Aurora Hinckley High School, University of Colorado 1985-1989.

The Denver Viners :: Irv Brown

Long before Title IX, Colorado had a terrific AAU women's basketball team called the Denver Viners. They took on all comers including the legendary Amarillo Queens of Wayland Baptist University. Other team names: Atlanta Tomboys and the Kansas City Dons. The Viners traveled a lot and were really entertaining. Here are my top five in order.

5. Jean McAndrews.
The ultimate team player.

4. Dorothy Majors.
She controlled the boards. Was married to the team's coach Les Majors.

3. Peggy Gibson.
From a great family, her husband Ben played AAU ball with the Central Bankers. Daughter Jaynie Gibson McHugh starred at Arvada West. Now coaches volleyball at San Francisco University.

2. Mugsie Walker.
Tremendous floor game. She was also a top-notch softball player.

1. Joanie Birkland.
One of the best women athletes from Denver ever. She had a great feel for the game. A tremendous all-around athlete, Joan won state tennis championships in 1960, 1961, 1962, 1965, and 1966. She is the currently the executive director of Sportswomen of Colorado, and is a member of the Colorado Sports of Hall of Fame.

Best Basketball Pros :: Jeff Bzdelik

Note: Jeff Bzdelik, head coach of men's basketball at CU, worked for more than a dozen years in the NBA. He was a long-time assistant to Pat Riley and was the head coach of the Denver Nuggets for three years. Nuggets fans will always love Bzdelik for coaching a young team to an impressive turnaround, leading them to the playoffs in 2003-04 for the first time since 1994-95. Before heading to CU, Jeff coached the Air Force Falcons. We asked Jeff to list the five all-time best pros.

5. John Stockton.
Greatest little point guard.

4. Magic Johnson.
Greatest big point guard.

3. Kareem Abdul Jabbar.
Sky hook.

2. Michael Jordan.
The best ever.

1. Larry Bird.
Total package.

Best Big Guys in Basketball :: Ervin Johnson

Note: Denver's Ervin Johnson was a 6-foot-11 center in the NBA—not to be confused with Earvin "Magic" Johnson, who was a guard. Ervin didn't play much basketball in high school. At age 20, he enrolled at the University of New Orleans and worked his way up to averaging 18.4 points and 11.9 rebounds per game during his senior year. Ervin finished his career at New Orleans as the school's all-time leader in rebounds and blocked shots. In the 1993 NBA draft, he was the 23rd pick overall. For 13 years, he played professionally with the Sonics, Timberwolves and Bucks. From 1996–97, he was a Denver Nugget. He now lives in Denver and is a community ambassador for the Denver Nuggets. The kids love him. He's a great communicator. We asked him to list the toughest big guys he covered in his career.

5. Tim Duncan.
All the moves. Great fundamentals.

4. Karl Malone. Strong.
Very clever. Great at getting position and drawing fouls.

3. Kevin Garnett.
Could shoot the 20-footer then take you on the dribble.

2. Hakeem "The Dream" Olajuwon.
So many moves he'd take you out on the floor and kill you with that fade-away.

1. Shaquille O'Neal.
Shaq. So big, but not that much skill. He's just a rock.

How's this for an obscure exercise: We've made three dream teams of the best–ever high school basketball players from the Denver Metro area, by position. These are the 15 top local men's basketball preps of all time.

Third Team

5. Jim Feeney.
Guard. Fairview HS. NBA All-Star Tom Chambers once said: "Feeney is better than any point guard he played with in the NBA."

4. Harry Hollins.
Guard. Manual HS. An All-American at DU. The lefty could really shoot with great range.

3. Ken Charlton.
Center. South HS. An All-American at CU who became a bank president.

2. Dave Logan.
Forward. Wheat Ridge HS. Solid career at CU. Drafted in three sports. Chose the NFL.

1. Michael Ruffin.
Forward. Cherry Creek HS. Starred at Tulsa. Still playing in the NBA.

Second Team

5. Michael Ray Richardson.
Guard. Manual HS. Starred at Montana then was all-pro with the Knicks. On the all-pro team four years.

4. Pat Frink.
Guard. Wheat Ridge HS. The best pure shooter from the state. He played at CU and with the Cincinnati Royals.

3. Chuck Darling.
Center. South. All-American at Iowa, then a star in AAU ball.

2. Hal Kinard.
Forward. West HS. Only six-foot, he was the best defender in high school. Same story at CSU where he was all WAC.

1. Mark Randall.
Forward. Cherry Creek HS. Played on a National championship team at Kansas. First-round pick of the Chicago Bulls.

First Team

5. Dennis Boone.

Guard. Manual HS. Perhaps the best jump shooter the city has seen. Had a great college career at Regis College.

4. Chauncey Billups.

Guard. George Washington HS. Was an All-American at CU. Still going strong for the Detroit Pistons.

3. Ron Shavlik.

Center. East HS. Earned All-American honors at North Carolina State. First-round pick by the Knicks.

2. Tom Chambers.

Forward. Fairview HS. Another guy who earned All-American honors at Utah. Had a nice career in the NBA.

1. Art Bunte.

Forward. South High School. Built like Mark Aguirre with a great touch. Went on to earn All-American honors at the University of Utah.

Bad Pickaxe Picks :: Chris Dempsey

Note: Chris Dempsey writes about the Nuggets for *The Denver Post*. Bonus factoid: Chris played high school basketball at Montbello. He lists the five biggest first-round flame-outs drafted in Nuggets history.

5. 1989: Todd Lichiti (No. 15).
Averaged a career-best 14.0 ppg in 1990-91.

4. 1991: Mark Macon (No. 8).
His game didn't translate to pros.

3. 1997: Tony Battie (No. 5).
"El Busto," meet Denver. Denver, "El Busto."

2. 1998: Raef LaFrentz (No. 3).
Four decent seasons. Never a star.

1. 2002: Nikoloz Tskitishvili (No. 5 overall).
Five years later, out of the league.

Irv Picks the Best College Basketball Coaches Ever in Colorado

There are so many great coaches to choose from—and Ceal Barry and Kathy McConnell-Miller come to mind. I'll narrow it down to men's coaches. Some of these picks may surprise you.

5. Bob Spears, Air Force Academy.

With all due respect: What Joe Scott and Jeff Bzdelik did, Major Spears was doing in the 60s at the old cadet gym. He ran the shuffle offense and got lay-up after lay-up.

3 and 4. Tie. Sox Walseth, CU and Jim Williams, CSU.

Sox beat them all in Old Balch, and out-coached the better-funded programs. Balanced the floor as good as anyone in the country. Jim Williams was the winingest coach in state history. He fought the battles when the Rams weren't in a league. As tough a competitor as you'll ever be around.

2. Boyd "Tiny" Grant, CSU.

He brought the school a WAC Conference championship—no easy task with BYU and Utah. He was still teaching the fundamentals in March.

1. Mike Dunlap, Metro State.

This will surprise you because he's not Division I. Won a couple of Division II national titles. I have refereed six NCAA Championship games. Mike stacks up with any coach. The full-court pressure, the shot selection, and above all, the commitment to excellence—just outstanding. I never saw the guy take a set or play off.

It Spells Trouble

Irv is notoriously bad with spelling and names. He's been known to confuse Roy Halladay and Matt Holliday, for instance. He knows so many people—and meets more daily—but his brain isn't getting any bigger. Our apologies to everyone whose name we mangled in this book. Please know: Even if we can't spell it or pronounce it, your name is engraved in our hearts. Here's a list of names in Colorado sports that have tripped up even the best spellers and namedroppers.

17. Hamza Abdullah.
Broncos safety.

16. Esse Baharmast.
Director of International Referees. Soccer.

15. Karlis Skrastins.
Defenseman, Avalanche.

14. Darren Drozdov.
Defensive tackle, Broncos.

13. Steve Konowalchuk.
Avalanche got him from Washington.

12. Robert Konovsky.
End, Broncos.

11. Anti Laaksonen.
Left winger, Avalanche.

10. Jim Szymanski.
Defensive end, Broncos.

9. David Marcinyshyn.
Avalanche, 1991.

8. Anton Palepoi.
Defensive end, Broncos.

7. Johnny Olszewski.
Broncos. "Johnny O."

6. Carl Schaukowitch.
Broncos guard.

5. Tariq Abdul Wahid.
Nuggets.

4. Mahmoud Abdul-Rauf.
Nuggets.

3. Nikoloz Tskitishvili.
Nuggets first-round draft pick.

2. Curtis Leschyshyn.
Quebec's first pick. Avalanche got him.

1. Sarunas Marciulionis.
Nuggets.

Johnsons We're Glad to See

A wise man once said: "You can't win without a Johnson." Here are 11 of our favorite notable, not-so-notable or never-heard-of-em Johnsons. You'll just have to take our word for it.

11. Pug.
When softball was big in Denver in the late 40s, Pug, Larry Bollig, Ray Weimer, Jim Sparkman and Ed Bezjak were dominating.

10. Big Ed.
President of the Old Western League.

9. Ervin.
"Not Magic." (Ervin, not Earvin.) Played for the Nuggets 1996-97. Averaged 7 points per game.

8. Howard.
Ho-Jo. One year with the Rockies, 1994. He had seen better days. Slow bat.

7. Charles.
Catcher for the Rockies 2003-2004.

6. Kyle.
The fullback from Syracuse. That guy takes on linebackers.

5. Marcia.
Marcia? Marcia! The Denver City Councilwoman and big Rockies fan. She and her husband took their grandson to Rockies spring training in Tucson. They expected to watch him expand his baseball-card and autograph collections. Instead, he stood just beyond the outfield fence during practice, shagging balls for hours on end. He proudly went home with 15 balls that are displayed in their unsigned glory in his room.

4. Butch.
Playing for Dallas in Super Bowl XII, he made a spectacular catch from Roger Staubach that helped the Cowboys beat the Broncos. Butch then played here in 1984-85.

3. Avery.
Played briefly for the Nuggets, was traded to Dallas and now is their coach.

2. Vance.
One of the Three Amigos. He could run. He also had 12 games where his receiving yards were 100 or better.

1. Charlie.
Before Morton and Elway, Charlie from New Mexico State gave you a chance in 1973. The Broncos went 7-5-2. Unheard of! Charlie threw 20 touchdown passes. Riley Odoms caught seven.

Note: John Hancock is the track coach at Mullen. His dad, Tom Hancock, was football coach at Lakewood High. John graduated from the University of Northern Colorado in 1977 and has been Mullen's head coach since 1986. He has directed ten boys' state championship teams, four state runner-ups, and three third-place finishes. We asked him to choose girls and boys to call the best in Colorado.

Girls

2005 Chelsea Taylor/Montbello.
Chelsea set two state records in winning the high jump at 6 feet one-half-inch and the long jump at 21 feet three-quarter inches. Both distances were considered close to the top marks in the country, and would be great college marks. She also ran great relay legs.

2004 Ashley Owens/Liberty.
Ashley ran the top times in Colorado for the sprints. She was the World Junior Champion in the 100 at 11.13, and had a best of 23.26 in the 200m. She dominated her events and ran marks that would be competitive with anyone in the world regardless of age.

2000 Twink Kranik/Highlands Ranch.
Twink set a state record at 41.35 in the 300H, and ran the most amazing 400 in the mile relay I have ever seen in Colorado. I loved her competitive nature and talent. I think her time in the hurdles led the nation that year.

1991 Melody Fairchild/Boulder.
She set a national indoor/outdoor record in 1991 in the 3000 9:55.91 and won state in a record 4:51.56 (mile).

1973 Wendy Koenig/Estes Park.
She ran 2:03.03 in a dual meet with East Germany in Munich when she was in high school. Wendy also set the world record at the time for the 400H in the same year with a time of 59.8. That would be hard to top.

Boys

2006 Jacob Scheuerman/Littleton.
He has the best time ever in the state for 400m at 46.23 in a rain storm at state, ran the 200m in 20.74, and the 100m in an impressive 10.39! The best set of times you will find.

2001 Gerren Crochet/Bear Creek-Boulder.
Gerren could have been competitive at any event. He ran the 300H in 36.41, a state record. But he could spring, do any jumping event. Great relay runner, and a class athlete.

1986 Pat Manson/Aurora Central.

Pat is still the state record holder in the pole vault, jumping an amazing 18 feet 0 inches. Won state in the long jump and was their lead off runner in the 4x1. He is the only U.S. vaulter to jump over 18 feet each year for two decades.

1982 Jim Banich/Arvada.

Jim still holds the top distances for the shot and discus, even though he was 6-foot-3 and 185, and could only bench press185. Jim threw the shot 68 feet 2.5 inches, and the discus 202 feet 1 inch. He was also the state champ in the 100 high hurdles.

Note: John Meyer writes about the Olympics for *The Denver Post.* We asked him to list great runners who went to school in Colorado. In no particular order.

Pat Porter.

Evergreen High School, Adams State. Won eight straight U.S. cross country titles, 1982-89. Two-time Olympian. Two-time NAIA champ.

Adam Goucher.

Doherty HS, University of Colorado. 1998 NCAA cross country champion. 1998 NCAA 5,000 meter champion. Two-time U.S. 5,000-meter champion. Three-time U.S. cross country champion. 2000 Olympian.

Melody Fairchild.

Boulder High School. Six-time Colorado prep champion. Two-time national (Foot Locker) cross country champion. First American high school girl to break 10 minutes for two miles; 1991 world junior cross country bronze medalist; 1996 NCAA 3,000-meter champion for Oregon.

Jon Sinclair.

Arvada West, Colorado State. Highly successful road racer of the 1980s who won the 1980 U.S. cross country title and 1984 U.S. 10,000 title. Former U.S. 5K record holder.

Dan Reese.

Wheat Ridge HS, University of Colorado. 1982 Irv Brown-Woody Paige athlete of the month. 1995 bronze medallist Pan Am Games steeplechase. 1991 world cross country team. 1987 Big Eight champion. Member of 12 U.S. national teams.

Elva Dryer.

Durango HS, Western State. Five-time Division II track champion. Two-time Division II cross country champion. Two-time Olympian.

Alan Culpepper.

University of Colorado. Two-time Olympian. Three-time U.S. champion on the track. 1996 NCAA 5,000-meter champion. Three-time U.S. cross country champion.

Dathan Ritzenhein.

University of Colorado. 2003 NCAA cross country champion. 2004 Olympian. American-born collegiate record holder for 10,000 meters, 2005 U.S. cross country champion.

Coloradans like to run, jog, walk and roll. You'll see 'em everywhere in all kinds of weather, racking up the miles. The Denver area has a lot of perennial fun runs and road races such as the Cherry Creek Sneak and Thanksgiving Turkey Trot to keep you moving. Here's a selection of our favorites.

5. Furry Scurry.

Your dogs will be barking after this one. It's an annual two-mile fun run for people and their canine companions in Washington Park. Great for kids. The event benefits the Denver Dumb Friends League and thousands of homeless and abandoned animals.

4. Runnin' of the Green.

This is a lucky 7K race. At the finish line, you'll find corned beef, Guinness and Irish dancing. Now that's what we call lucky. Denver is home to one of the largest St. Patrick's Day celebrations in the nation. Runnin' of the Green is part of the annual festivity in Lower Downtown. Slainte mah.

3. Colfax Marathon.

A marathon is 26.2 miles long. Colfax Avenue, said to be the longest avenue in America, is 26 miles long. You can see the bulb lighting up over someone's head: Let's have a Colfax Marathon. Inaugurated in 2006, this event is still working out the glitches. In 2007, the course was measured incorrectly and runners ended up going 26.7 miles by the time they crossed the finish line. A new course—highlighting the diverse scenic appeal of Colfax from Aurora to Lakewood through Denver—was introduced in 2008. It was a big hit in 2008, with more than 5,000 participants. We hope this race becomes a beloved local tradition. Colfax isn't nearly as seedy as we like to remember it.

2. Race for the Cure.

It's like a mass demonstration against breast cancer in the Pepsi Center parking lot. In 2007, more than 60,000 people participated in the 5K run/walk on a route along Speer, Federal and Colfax. The event raises around $3 million for breast cancer research. It's sometimes solemn, as participants remember loved ones lost to cancer. It's also inspiring to see survivors of the disease rallying. If you can't drag yourself out of bed, you can sign up to Sleep in for the Cure, and catch extra Zzzs on race day.

1. Bolder Boulder.

The most famous and fun road run in Colorado. Some people have done it every Memorial Day since 1979. In 2006, the event was the fifth largest road race in the world, bigger than the New York City marathon. Participants—many in costume—hit the 6.2-mile course through the streets of Boulder, ending up at a big bash of about 90,000 people at the University of Colorado's Folsom Field. Elite runners from around the world come to compete. Race officials estimate that 30,000 spectators line the streets to cheer. Each year, the event brings Boulder a $10 million economic boost. That's something.

Five Places to Run

The city of Denver is home to around 200 parks. Here are a few good places to get in shape for a race or just get some air.

5. Rocky Mountain Lake Park.

The footpath around the lake is less than a mile roundtrip, eight tenths of a mile to be exact. A great place to work up to an extra lap or two. Wear mosquito repellent around sunrise or sunset when the weather is warm. At 46th and Hooker.

4. Cherry Creek Trail.

This 12.8-mile path follows the creek all the way from I-225 to Confluence Park. The downtown segment from Broadway to Confluence Park is about three miles. Lots of bicycles on this path. Watch out.

3. Cheesman Park.

Check out the mountain views and huge old trees. Believe it or not, this was the site of Denver's first cemetery. They moved the bodies of course—most of them, anyway. The dirt path around the perimeter is a 1.6 mile loop. At 8th and Franklin.

2. Washington Park.

The path around the perimeter is 2.35 miles. The paved path is 2.27 miles around. This has gotta be the most beautiful park in the city. In summertime, the flowerbeds are stunning. Now you know we have a sensitive side. At E. Louisiana and S. Downing.

1. Sloan's Lake.

The concrete path around the lake is 2.9 miles. It's a good, uninterrupted path for a longer walk or jog. We think there's a "lake effect;" when the wind is chilly, it's chillier around Sloan's. Legend is, a farmer named Sloan went out to dig a well. Somehow, a large lake formed where he tapped the water table. Oops. At 26th and Stuart or 17th and Sheridan.

Note: John lists athletes who didn't go to school in Colorado but are great international runners and long-time residents of the state. In no particular order.

Frank Shorter.
Boulder. 1972 Olympic marathon champion. 1976 Olympic silver medal in marathon. Five-time U.S. 10,000-meter champion. Four-time U.S. cross country champion.

Mark Plaatjes.
Boulder. 1993 marathon world champion.

Arturo Barrios.
Boulder. Former world record holder, 10,000 meters.

Steve Jones.
Boulder. Former world record holder, marathon.

Colleen De Reuck.
Boulder. 2002 world cross country bronze medallist. Four-time Olympian. Two-time U.S. cross country champion.

Lorraine Moller.
Boulder. Four-time Olympian for New Zealand, including bronze medal in marathon, 1992.

Matt Carpenter.
Manitou Springs. One of America's premier mountain runners with eight Pikes Peak marathon wins and six Pikes Peak Ascent wins. Course record holder in the Leadville 100.

Every ball club has to have a character—someone who keeps you loose. We've had our share in Denver, but these two stand out.

2. Glen Gondrezick.

Denver Nuggets, 1979-1983. Gondo was a star at Boulder High School. He went on to play for Jerry Tarkanian at UNLV. He was an all-out guy who made a living playing defense and diving after loose balls. His Rebel team went to the Final Four in 1977. I was the referee in the semi-final game vs. North Carolina. I called Gondo for three charging fouls. He didn't speak to me for a long time. Glen was drafted by the Knicks and wound up in Denver in 1979. He was extremely popular with the fans and a favorite of Coach Doug Moe. He was a cut-up, particularly with the trainer, Chopper Travaglini. My favorite Gondo story: We were waiting for our luggage in Philadelphia. The bags were coming down, and out of the chute came Gondo. I don't know how he got in the chute but the travelers waiting for their luggage got a kick out of it. With security the way it is now, he couldn't have pulled it off. Glen lives in Las Vegas and works for a casino. He also does UNLV games on radio.

1. Fran Lynch.

Fran was drafted by the Broncos in 1967 out of Hofstra. He was picked in the fifth round, 110th in the draft. That was the first year that the NFC and AFC had an agreement to merge. Denver's first pick that year was Floyd Little. Fran served as his backup. He played until 1976. John Ralston was the head coach and Fran drove him nuts. Ralston was a cheerful, earnest optimist. Everything was great—the glass was always half full. John had the special teams huddled up for a pep talk. He said, "I wish I could go down on this kick-off with you." Lynch took off his helmet and handed it to John and said "Go ahead, take my place." After his football days, Fran did Bronco Talk after the games on KOA. The show featured a lot of callers who might have had too much alcohol. He was a classic. Fran still lives in Denver and works for the Ingram Sports Network.

Note: Mike Spence has covered sports for the Pueblo Chieftain for 16 years. He was a very good cross-country runner himself at Pueblo Centennial. Colorado Springs has had some solid athletes. Mike lists some of the very best, in no particular order.

Vincent Jackson.
Widefield High School wideout. Now a future star with the San Diego Chargers.

Aaron Smith.
Sierra High School. Now a star defensive end with the Pittsburgh Steelers.

Terry Miller.
Mitchell High School. Starred at Oklahoma State and the Buffalo Bills.

Jim Smith.
Wasson High School. Played at Air Force.

James Hill.
Widefield High School. Led the state in rushing. Played at CU and the Oakland Raiders.

Ted Castaneda.
Wrestling and cross-country.

Jeff King.
Rampart High School. Number one pick out of Arkansas of the Kansas City Royals.

Goose Gossage.
Wasson High School. One of the best relief pitchers ever.

Cullen Bryant.
Wasson High School. A Defensive back at CU who became a star running back for the L.A. Rams.

G.B. Funk.
Two-sport coach at Wasson High School. Is in the Colorado Sports Hall of Fame.

Justin Armour.
Manitou Springs High School. Starred at Stanford, played for the Denver Broncos.

Adam Goucher.
Nationally ranked distance runner.

Note: Author and journalist Terry Frei is a columnist for *The Denver Post*. His books include *'77: Denver, the Broncos, and a Coming of Age*, and *Third Down & A War to Go*. Here he lists the most memorable events in Avalanche history.

10. The sellout streak.

On November 9, 1995, the Avalanche announced a sellout for their eighth regular-season game ever, a 1-1 tie with Dallas as McNichols Sports Arena. For the next 11 years, the team, at least officially, sold out every home game. A huge season-ticket list, with a waiting list, provided a cushion, and there inevitably were many no-shows for some games, but there was no questioning the fact that the NHL became a hot ticket. Done in by what was perceived to be a regression on ice, wince-inducing prices (the Avalanche weren't alone on that) and the lingering effect of the 2004-05 lost season, the streak came to an end at 487 games, with a non-sellout for the Avalanche's 5-3 loss to Chicago on October 16, 2006. Record keeping on such things was spotty in the NHL's past, and colloquially it often has been said that Toronto hasn't had an unsold seat since World War II. But the Avalanche streak was the longest recorded one in NHL history.

9. The arrival and unfortunate departure of Chris Drury.

He was the chubby kid pitching the team from Trumbull, Connecticut, to the Little League World Series championship in Williamsport, Pennsylvania. He chose hockey, instead, and won the Hobey Baker Award, hockey's Heisman, as NCAA hockey's top player at Boston University in 1998. He was an almost afterthought, but shrewd, choice in the 1994 draft by the Nordiques. And when Chris Drury left BU and signed with the Avalanche, he was an immediate sensation. He won the Calder Trophy in 1999. It wasn't that he piled up goals, and he had "only" 85 in his four full seasons with Colorado. Rather, it was his knack to score clutch goals, especially in the playoffs, that endeared him to Colorado fans. Dating back to his Little League experience, it also was clear that he had that ineffable quality of a winner. But that wasn't enough for the Avs, who traded him to Calgary in October 2002, and many considered it a dark day for the franchise that started a slide.

8. Todd Bertuzzi's assault on Steve Moore.

This was a black eye for hockey and, to a very minor degree, for the Avalanche organization. Moore was a Harvard-educated forward from the Toronto suburbs who had caught on with the Avs as a checking-line center, and he seemed to be destined to have at least a decent career as a utility-type player in the league. That ended on March 8, 2004. There was some history to this, of course, including Moore's open-ice hit on Vancouver captain Markus Naslund in a February game in Denver. Naslund suffered facial bruises and a mild concussion as the result of the unpenalized hit. If it had been a similar hit delivered on Joe Sakic or Peter Forsberg by a marginal Canucks player, of course, the hue and cry in Denver would have been major. In Vancouver, because it was a Canucks star and an Avs role player, you'd have thought Moore had gone after Naslund with a machete. After the game that night, Bertuzzi said that it was too bad that the game had been close, and we inferred that Moore would have been targeted for retribution if the game had been out of hand. And in the same locker room, Canucks winger Brad May mused that there might be a "bounty" on Moore. The teams met again in Denver in the first week of March. And what happened? Nothing. Of course, it didn't matter that commissioner Gary Bettman just happened to be in attendance. But in Vancouver five days later, with the Avalanche winning a blowout in the third period, Bertuzzi stalked Moore, sucker punched him from behind and drove him into the ice. Moore suffered three fractured neck vertebrae, a concussion, and facial abrasions. It was the last NHL game he ever played. Bertuzzi was suspended for the rest of the regular season and the playoffs, a sentence that added up to 20 games. One reason for that was that the NHL was dark for the 2004-05 season because of the lockout, but he was back for the 2005-06 season. Moore's contract with the Avalanche ran out, and as of late 2007, his lawsuit against Bertuzzi and the Canucks' ownership was pending in Ontario. The Avalanche drew some criticism, and much of it justified, for their seemingly cavalier treatment of Moore after being in his corner during the initial stages of his hospitalization and rehabilitation. The Avs' ill-fated signing of May was hard to stomach, and although it was obvious the league had made it clear it would prefer the organization distance itself from someone suing another league franchise and a player, Colorado would have shown considerable courage—and class—by thumbing noses at that and publicly standing with Moore. It didn't.

7. Pierre Lacroix's reign.

He wasn't perfect. He made mistakes. But there was no disputing that the former player agent-turned-GM was the major force behind the Avalanche making Denver a hockey town, pulling of the trades for—among others—Roy, Borque, and Blake. His modus operandi was not to work the free-agent market, but rather to make deals for potential "rental" players at the deadline and then decide whether to re-sign them. It worked most of the time, despite the ill-fated Theo Fleury deal. One of the knocks against Lacroix from jealous folks around the league—that he was free-spending GM with an unlimited budget—was absurd. The Avs were near the top in payroll, but he always had a budget, especially in the early days of the franchise and in the shaky days of the evolving ownership group that eventually passed the franchise on to Stan Kroenke. He stepped back a bit in 2006, becoming team president only and turning the GM job over to Francois Giguere.

6. Patrick Roy becomes No. 1.

Roy was driven, above all, to win. As equipment changed, as rules changed, as players and standards of statistical evaluation changed, one thing remained the same. If you let in fewer goals than the guy at the other end, your team won. That was the bottom line for Roy, in the postseason, but also in the relentless grind of the regular season. So he went after Terry Sawchuk's long-standing record of 447 regular-season victories with a single-minded passion. And he passed Sawchuk when the Avalanche beat the Capitals 4-3 in overtime in Washington on October 17, 2000. Peter Forsberg tipped in Ray Bourque's shot from the point to win it, and within seconds, Roy was riding on the shoulders of his teammates, and it wasn't long before he was taking a congratulatory phone call from Canadian Prime Minister Jean Chretien. "I saw Ray (Bourque) taking the shot, and I knew t was going wide," Roy said that night. "When Peter put his stick on it, it was fun to see it go in . . . I think it's hard to appreciate it now as much as I will in a couple of years when I retire and have more time to think about it. Or maybe even tomorrow, when I lay down and I have more time to relax." He had 551 victories when he retired, and it remains his top regular-season accomplishment. Of course, his four Stanley Cup celebrations, two in Montreal and two in Colorado, are his signature.

5. The height of the Red Wings-Avalanche Rivalry.

Where did it begin? Well, that's a matter for debate, and in some ways it began in the Avalanche's first game in Denver, a rather mild and uneventful Avs win over the Red Wings in McNichols Sports Arena. It began that night because it was clear that these might be the two best teams in the Western Conference, a significant point because the Nordiques had been in the Eastern Conference, and this was going to be a match up with even more significant ramifications down the road. But it really hot heated as the Avalanche were pulling off the six-game upset of the Red Wings in the Western Conference finals. In the final game, Colorado winger Claude Lemieux, the kind of guy you loved to have on your team, but hated when he was wearing the opposition sweater, checked Detroit center Kris Draper from behind (or the side, depending on your perspective) and drove him head-first into the boards. Draper suffered horrific facial injuries. After the game, Red Wings winger Dino Ciccarelli said of Lemieux: "I can't believe I shook his freakin' hand." (One of the "funny" aspects was that Ciccarelli really said just that, censoring himself.) When the Avalanche went on to win the Cup, and both Draper and his teammates felt as if Lemieux neither displayed remorse nor sufficiently apologized, and the emotional stakes were raised. It led to an infamous March 26, 1997 game in Joe Louis Arena, when Darren McCarty, Draper's linemate and long-time friend, went after Lemieux and pummeled him, and all hell broke loose around them. Inexplicably, referee Paul Devorski didn't toss McCarty out of the game, it would have been easy for him to exercise what is acknowledged as discretionary power to head off further trouble, even if that meant making up a reason to give Lemieux a game misconduct as well, and McCarty ended up scoring the game-winning goal in overtime of a fight-filled game. And, oh, yes, one of the fights during all of this featured Roy going at it with Red Wings goalie Mike Vernon. The rivalry, thus heated up, became notorious for the wrong reasons. For much of the time, it was the two (of the) best teams in the league, but the television staples became the mayhem that came in that March 26 game and in others that followed throughout the next few seasons. By 2007, the rivalry still exists, but with nowhere near the enmity of the late 1990s.

4. Foppa and Super Joe . . . or is that Super Joe and Foppa?

When the franchise arrived from Quebec, the Avalanche already had a premier 1-2 center punch, young captain Sakic and the baby-faced Swede, Forsberg, who was coming off a season in which he won the Calder Trophy as the league's rookie of the year. Quebec had landed Forsberg's rights as part of the trade that sent Erick Lindros' rights to the Flyers, and it was a deal that would prove to be fortuitous for Colorado fans. Having both Sakic and Forsberg forced other teams to make pick-your-poison choices, both in the era when checking lines were in vogue, and also when the match up strategy became more about sending your top defensive pairing out against a top line. It worked for the Avs, despite what turned out to be Forsberg's physical problems. They both could be worth the (very expensive) price of admission on separate nights, with Forsberg checking the "soft Swede" stereotype into the boards, bracing for or inviting hits, and often giving back the same thing. He seemingly couldn't be knocked off the puck, and his late-season performance in the 2002-03 season, with all due respect Sakic and Roy, remains the top individual run in franchise history. He had a league-high 77 assists and 106 points, and won the Hart Trophy as the league's MVP. And Sakic? He had won the Hart two years earlier, and deservingly so. He is a different kind of player, too, with a wicked wrist shot and an ability to either avoid or mitigate the damage from hits, and his quiet, but humor-filled, leadership was a crucial element in the Avalanche's success. For nine season, Colorado fans had it great, watching the Forsberg and Sakic show, but the realities of the salary-cap era, and the timing of contracts, led to Forsberg's departure and signing with Philadelphia after the lockout ended. It was fun while it lasted. [This was written before Forsberg returned to the Avs in February 2008.]

3. The 1996 Stanley Cup Run.

It was Colorado's first major-league championship, and there never could be another first. For that alone, it was notable, but the gradually building excitement as this market became familiar with this team as it progressed from championship-caliber to championship-winning was something to behold. In the Western Conference half of the playoff draw, the Avalanche knocked off, in succession, Vancouver, Chicago, and Detroit, and then swept the Florida Panthers in an anticlimactic Stanley Cup Finals. Perhaps this sounds strange now, but the Western Conference semifinal against the Blackhawks remains, as of this writing, the most entertaining playoff series in Avalanche history. Colorado won in six games, but there were many nervous moments and a lot of fun along the way. The Blackhawks, featuring American-born forwards Jeremy Roenick and Tony Amonte, and goalie Ed Belfour, earned a split of the first two games in Denver, won Game 3 in Chicago and were on the verge of taking a stranglehold on the series when Game 4 went to overtime in the United Center. Andy Van Hellemond, the veteran referee, was about to retire. In the third overtime, he was Avalanche defenseman Sandis Ozolinsh haul Roenick down from behind as the Blackhawks' star was breaking in on Roy. It should have been a penalty shot for Roenick. Or, at the very least, a minor penalty on Ozolinsh, which would have given the Hawks a power play. Van Hellemond swallowed his whistle and called nothing, and the Avalanche went on to win the game on Joe Sakic's goal in the third overtime. That swung the momentum, and Colorado advanced after winning Game 5 in Denver and Game 6 (again in overtime) at Chicago. Along the way, the entertaining byplay between Roy and Roenick spiced things up. After Game 4, Roenick claimed he would have ended the game if he had been awarded a penalty shot, and the next day, Roy responded to the media that we should tell Roenick that he couldn't hear him because Roy's two Stanley Cup rings were plugging his ears. Colorado's victory over the Red Wings was especially notable because Detroit had just roared through a 62-13-7 regular season, and their 131 points were 27 more than the league's second-best total, the Avalanche's 104. Then came the strange conclusion, the Avalanche's sweep of the Panthers, ending after midnight in Miami when Uwe Krupp finally scored the overtime goal that gave Colorado a 1-0 victory in Game 4. And the celebration was on in Denver, culminating in the downtown parade and celebration outside the City and County Building. The official crowd estimate of 450,000 might have been generous, but there was no doubting the magnitude of the exhilaration.

2. Trade for Patrick Roy.

On December 6, 1995, the Avalanche were in the early stages of their first season in Denver, when they announced they had picked up the veteran goalie from the Montreal Canadiens. In retrospect, it was the deal that put the NHL over the top in Denver. It came off because of Roy's volatility and also a curious refusal in Montreal, both among the Canadiens organization and the media, to forgive and forget his angry reaction during a Detroit-Montreal game the previous weekend in the Forum. Canadiens coach Mario

Tremblay, Roy's one-time road roommate, left him in for nine Detroit goals during the Red Wings' 11-1 romp, and Roy finally was summoned to the bench, the goalie reacted petulantly. But the funny thing was, in retrospect, was that it wasn't profane or even high-decibel. Roy squeezed past Tremblay on the bench, approached team president Ronald Corey and hissed, in French, that he had played his last game in Montreal. The moment was captured on television, of course, and replayed about a million times, but what was the big deal? Clearly, the Canadiens and now general manager Rejean Houle felt as if Roy wouldn't be good in a rebuilding situation, and this probably represented an excuse to do what they might have ended up doing, anyway. But after a couple of days of Roy limbo, Roy and team captain Mike Keane were sent to the Avalanche for Andrei Kovalenko, Martin Rucinsky, and Jocelyn Thibault. The planets were aligned on this one, too: Avalanche general manager Pierre Lacroix had been Roy's agent before switching sides of the table, and there was no way the Canadiens would have traded him to the Nordiques, their provincial rivals. But with the franchise relocated to Denver, the deal was possible, and if the truth be told, the view at the time was that sending someone to Colorado, even if it was to join a team on the rise, still was closer to exiling a guy than granting him a wish. Roy wouldn't beg for forgiveness in Montreal. "It was clear from the organization that they had made their decision," he said a few days after joining the Avalanche. "I said, "Ok, I'll accept my mistake. I agree I was the one who made that thing happen on that Saturday and both parties agreed it was in the best interests of us that we go different directions." "I understand that you can't put 10 years aside and give it a little tap and it's all gone. I lived through lots of good things in Montreal, but, again, it's a turn I accept. This will be a very nice experience for us." He turned out to be right.

1. The 2001 Stanley Cup Run.

In some ways, this was a more genuine celebration, because by the team's sixth season in Denver, the community "knew" the Avalanche and was far more heavily invested in the on-ice fate of the franchise. A boom in youth hockey, largely attributable to the excitement the Avalanche created, was well underway, and thousands of kids in the area owned Avalanche replica jerseys with the names of their favorite players on the back. And in retrospect especially, the talent-laden nature of the Colorado roster at the time was remarkable. In 2000, the Avs had landed Ray Bourque from Boston in a trade, and when the Avalanche lost in seven games in the Western Conference finals to Dallas for the second year in a row, he soon announced he would be back for one more try to win the Stanley Cup. In 2001, near the trading deadline, Colorado acquired Rob Blake from the Kings. The pieces were there, and they came together in 2001, not without some drama. The Kings took the Avs to seven games in the Western Conference semifinals, and that night, Peter Forsberg announced at the Denver Chop House that he wasn't feeling good, and he underwent emergency surgery to remove his lacerated spleen. (Ouch.) After beating the Joel Quenneville-coached St. Louis Blues in the conference finals, the Avs, minus Forsberg, went up against the powerful New Jersey Devils in the Cup Final. They were on the ropes, down 3-2, heading into Game 6 in New Jersey, but sparked by a pep talk from Bourque and a terrific game from Patrick Roy, they won that, then got two goals from Alex Tanguay in Game 7 in Denver . . . and the celebration was on again. This time, much of the hockey world was cheering, too, because it signaled a triumphant end to Bourque's career, and the shots and video of him letting loose with a yell when raising the Cup, captain Joe Sakic quickly handed it off to him, remain memorable.

Irv Picks the Best Buffs Who Went Pro

The University of Colorado has graduated some outstanding athletes. Here are Irv's top ten Buffs-turned-pros:

10. Dick Anderson.
A great college player and an even better pro. Great career with the Miami Dolphins. Not a bad golfer either.

9. Boyd Dowler.
Made the move from single-wing blocking back to wideout. Remember Ray Scott, voice of the Packers in the Lombardi era: "Starr to Dowler. Touchdown."

8. Rashaan Salaam.
The Hiesman Trophy Winner. The best of the modern tailbacks. Chicago Bears' first-round pick in the 1995 NFL draft.

7. Carroll Hardy.
The guy who pinch-hit for Ted Williams was a great single wing tailback. Played for the Red Sox, Twins, Indians.

6. Cliff Branch.
Speed, speed, and more speed. And a marvelous personality. Three Super Bowl rings with the Raiders.

5. Bo Matthews.
The best blocking fullback I have seen. Top draft pick by the San Diego Chargers in 1974.

4. Michael Westbrook.
As good an athlete as you'll ever see, and tough. Played for the Redskins and Bengals. After the NFL he was in the Ultimate Fighting Group.

3. Bobby Anderson.
The face of the Buffaloes. A true All-American. Drafted in the first round in 1970. Played for the Broncos, Patriots, Redskins.

2. Alfred Williams.
His strength and quickness were special. Nobody could block him in college. Played for the Bengals, 49ers, Broncos.

1. Byron White.
"Whizzer" is the greatest scholar-athlete the country has ever had. The first $100,000 player in the NFL. Played for Pittsburgh and the Detroit Lions.

Bonus: Dave Logan.
Put him anywhere you want. Drafted in three sports, by NFL, NBA and MLB. Amazing. Seven years with the Cleveland Browns. He never dropped a pass.

Best Denver Pro Players Not Born in the U.S.A.

Some of our all-time favorites are imported classics.

10. Milan Hejduk.
Czech Republic. He won the Stanley Cup with Colorado in 2001. Won the Richard Trophy in 2002 and 2003. We like his style.

9. Adam Foote.
Canada. We hated it when he signed with Columbus. He gave the club toughness. He was special for Canada in the 1998 Olympics in Nagano, Japan. Glad he's back in Denver.

8. Vinny Castilla.
This guy from Mexico was a steal by Bob Gebhardt in the Rockies expansion draft. Nobody could throw the fastball by him.

7. Rob Blake.
Canada. What a break when we picked this guy up from LA in a trade for Adam Deadmarsh. Tough defenseman, very popular. Sorry to see him leave.

6. Jeff Francis.
Colorado Rockies. This Canadian lefty won 17 games for the club and he's just scratched the surface. He reminds us a lot of Sid Fernandez. Very hard to follow.

5. Peter Forsberg.
The Swede. We're thrilled he's an Av again. He has maybe the best ability of anyone on the ice. If only he could stay healthy. His picture is on a stamp in Sweden. Peter The Great.

4. Andres Galarraga, Rockies.
"The Big Cat" from Venezuela. Tremendously popular, and courageous—he whipped cancer. Could hit and field.

3. Dikembe Mutombo.
The best shot-blocker the Nuggets ever had plus he kept it alive. Our biggest problem with him is that he would rebound and shake his elbows to make sure the stat crew recorded it. By then the fast break opportunity was done. Does humanitarian work on behalf of his native Democratic Republic of Congo, formerly Zaire.

2. Patrick Roy.
Another Canadian inducted into the Hockey Hall of Fame. A great leader and ambassador of the game. Adored by Denver fans. His passion and determination was second to none.

1. Joe Sakic.
From Burnaby, British Columbia. Eighteen years with the Colorado Avalanche. No other player has been with the same team that long. Team captain for 14 years. People respect him and admire his community involvement.

Call it peanut butter meets chocolate, oil meets vinegar, Irv meets Joe. We're talking about two great players who play great together . . . or separately . . . or two guys who are somehow linked in some way having something to do with sports. Whatever. Here are our top ten dynamic duos.

10. Frank Tripucka and Lionel Taylor, Broncos.

The Tripper came here to coach. The Broncos didn't have a quarterback so they turned to Frank and he had some solid years. The guy he threw to, Taylor, finished his Broncos career as the franchise's all-time leader in receptions with 543.

9. Fat Leever and T.R. Dunn, Nuggets.

A most unlikely duo. Fat was a point guard who really wasn't; at six-foot-three, Fat was the Nuggets' leading rebounder. Dunn was the shooting guard who couldn't shoot. What he did was play defense and rebound. Irv used to get a kick out of the opponent fouling him late in the game. Never saw Dunn miss a free throw late in the game. Fun to watch.

8. Dennis Smith and Steve Atwater, Broncos.

These two, both at safety for the Broncos, were big hitters. Atwater was voted to a record seven consecutive Pro Bowls. When Denver won their first Super Bowl, he was brilliant. Smith, 14 years in the league, was All-AFC four times. He played on three Super Bowl teams. These two were a great pair of players.

7. M&M Connection, Craig Morton and Haven Moses, Broncos.

Craig and Haven were both inducted in the Colorado Sports Hall of Fame and the Bronco Ring of Fame at the same time. Morton came to Denver in a trade with the Giants in 1977. Led the team to the best record ever at the time, 12-2. Haven played 10 years and finished number three all-time receiver.

6. Hardy and Bernardi, CU Buffaloes football.

Carroll Hardy, the preacher, is the best all-around athlete CU ever produced. He went on to play pro football with the 49ers and Major League Baseball with the Red Sox. He's the guy who pinch-hit for Ted Williams. Hardy was the tailback and Frank Bernardi was the wingback in Dal Ward's single-wing offense. Bernardi blocked the extra point in the Missouri game that some still talk about. In 1960, the Denver Broncos first year, Bernardi was a starting cornerback.

5. Troy Tulowitski and Kazuo Matsui, Rockies.

Only together one year, but what a year: 2007 and the World Series. Tulo and Kaz were ·a great double-play combo. Fans wish Matsui wouldn't have signed with Houston. He was a great tablesetter.

4. Alex English and Dan Issel, Nuggets.

Both in the Hall of Fame. Alex, the all-time leading Nuggets scorer, was a great go-to guy. Issel, "The Horse" with the two missing front teeth, would take a big guy outside, give him a little junior high fake and take it to the hole.

3. Carmelo Anthony and Allan Iverson, Nuggets.

They've only been together two years but they have amazing skills. Melo is young. A.I. can take care of himself. Will they be better than the next two?

2. John Elway and Shannon Sharpe, Broncos.

Elway threw 300 touchdowns to 41 different receivers. The guy who caught the most was Sharpe with 42. Shannon also got a Super Bowl ring with Indy.

1. Ace Gruenig and Jumpin' Jack McCracken, AAU Nuggets.

Played for Denver Safeway (winners of the 1937 AAU championship) and original Nuggets. Ace mastered the hook shot and was an outstanding rebounder. McCracken could really jump. He mastered a flip of the wrist with a two-hander. McCracken was among the greatest players of all time in the AAU. Both Ace and Jack are in the Colorado Sports Hall of Fame.

How The Drive Went Down

The Drive. Yadda yadda. Blah blah blah. Is The Drive the only thing Broncos fans ever talk about? Yes, it is. The Drive is a tale of mythic heroism, a story to remind us that the impossible can become possible. When your buddy is at the end of his rope, you say, "How 'bout The Drive. That was something, wasn't it?" Then, suddenly, life is better. In fact, a little bluebird lands on your shoulder and sings a glad song while elves fold your laundry. Happens all the time when The Drive is mentioned. Here's the list of plays that took the Broncos 98-and-a-half yards in four minutes and 55 seconds back on that cold January day in Cleveland in 1987. Warms our hearts just to think of it.

15. First and ten on the Denver two.
John Elway completes a five-yard pass to Sammy Winder.

14. Winder runs three yards to the Broncos 10.
13. Winder picks up two more yards on a run.
Gets the first down.

12. Winder runs three more.
Ball is now on the Broncos 15.

11. Elway runs 11 yards.
10. Elway completes a 22-yard pass to Steve Sewell.
9. Elway gets the Broncos into Browns territory with a 12-yard pass to Steve Watson.
Oh man.

8. Elway's pass is incomplete.
Uh-oh. Ball is on the Browns 40.

7. Elway is sacked back to the Browns 48.
Whoa-no.

6. Elway connects with Mark Jackson for 20 yards, down to the Browns 28.
Holy moly.

5. Incomplete pass.
4. Sewell catches Elway's pass for 14 yards.
3. Incomplete pass.
Still on the Browns 14.

2. Elway scrambles nine yards to the Browns 5.
1. Elway passes to Jackson.
Five yards. Touchdown. Rich Karlis kicks the extra point to tie. Fans go wild. The game wasn't over, of course. Karlis made a field goal in overtime to win it. Great story. Timeless. Never gets old.

Jim "Tank" Turner

Although Jim "Tank" or "High Tops" Turner played QB at Utah State, he established himself as one of the leading kickers in pro football. The New York Jets signed him in 1964. He played with Joe Namath and kicked a record 34 field goals in 1968. In 1969, Jim kicked three field goals in the Jets' Super Bowl III victory over the Colts. He came to Denver in 1970 and has stayed here ever since. With the Broncos, Jim scored 742 points. He was the team's all-time leading scorer until Jason Elam surpassed that total in 1999. In his career, Jim scored 1,439 points, including 304 of 488 field goals (62%) and 521 of 534 extra points. Impressive stuff. We asked Jim to name the best kicker ever. He said: Jan Stenerud, the Norwegian "sharpshooter" who played for the Chiefs, Packers and Vikings. Jim retired from the Broncos in 1979. Here are a few of Jim's big plays with the Broncos that we'll never forget.

4. Jim's field goal to beat Oakland after John Matuszak said, "I'll break your back."

3. The sudden-death overtime kick in Atlanta.

2. The first Monday Night Football game in Denver: With seconds left, Jim hit a three-pointer vs. Oakland to tie up the game.

1. Jim's most memorable score was the time the Broncos faked a field goal and passed to Jim, who ran down the left sideline for the touchdown.

The Denver Broncos went to their first Super Bowl in 1977, thanks in large part to the Orange Crush defense. The team that had only two winning seasons since its inception in 1960 went 12 and 2 in 1977. Sales of t-shirts sporting the logo of the orange-flavored soft drink boomed in Denver. Orange Crush remains the single best nickname for a defense in this town. There were only four coaches but they were special. Joe Collier was the coordinator. Stan Jones had the down linemen. Myrel Moore had the linebackers. The late Richie McKay had the secondary. Collier was brilliant with his schemes. The talent had great chemistry. No book of Denver Sports Lists would be complete without the names of the Orange Crush, in no particular order.

Defensive End Lyle Alzado.
Hard to coach during the week, then on Sunday he was a blowtorch. Hyper. A real playmaker. Came out of Yankton College in South Dakota. Yankton is Tom Brokaw's hometown. Similarities to Brokaw end there.

Nose Guard Ruben Carter.
When you play the three-four defense, the most important spot is the nose guard. Ruben couldn't be blocked. They had to double-team him and that freed up the backers.

Defensive End Barney Chavous.
Consistent. Played the left side. Most teams are right handed and ran at Barney. He answered the challenge.

Linebacker Tom Jackson.
The fastest of the four backers. An outstanding blitzer, he could cover backs on pass patterns.

Linebacker Joe Rizzo.
The meanest of the backers. Always growling. He was mad at everyone including his teammates.

Linebacker Randy Gradishar.
Never missed a game. If they stayed in-bounds he found them. Gradishar is in the Ring of Fame. How come he's not in the NFL Hall of Fame? He oughtta be.

Linebacker Bob Swenson.
Just a sweetheart. Had to take on the tight end. He had the speed to cover backs on pass patterns.

Defensive Back Louie Wright.
A great cover corner. "Louie, here's your man. Shut him down." He was big and a great tackler.

Defensive Back Bernard Jackson.
Came over from Cincinnati. Played corner and safety. Good speed. Good tackler.

Defensive Back Steve Foley.
The corner moved to safety was a real ballhawk. All-time leader in picks.

Defensive Back Bill Thompson.
The leader in the secondary. Studied film more than anyone. When the projector was turned on Billy was in the front row.

Best Broncos by the Numbers

In our opinion, here are the best Denver Broncos by number from 1960 to the present.

99. Monte Reagor. DL, 1999-2002.
Undersized, played hard.

98. Rickey Hunley. LB, 1984-1987.
Went on to coach.

97. Mike Lodish. DL, 1995-2000.
Very steady.

96. Harold Hasselback. DL, 1994-2000.
Steady.

97. Marco Coleman. DL, 2005.
Best days behind him.

96. Keith Traylor. DL 1991-2000.
Was a linebacker.

93. Trevor Pryce. DL, 1997-2005.
We still miss him.

92. Bertrand Berry. DL, 2001-2003.
Sack man.

91. Alfred Williams. DL, 1996-1999.
Quick off the ball.

90. Neil Smith. DL, 1997.
Got a Super Bowl ring.

89. Orson Mobley. TE, 1986-1990.
Ran a nice drag pattern.

88. Clarence Kay. TE, 1984-1991.
They'd line him up at fullback.

87. Rich Jackson. DL, 1967-1972.
The Sheriff in the Ring of Fame.

86. Byron Chamberlin. TE, 1995-2000.
Blocker.

85. Ron Egloff. TE, 1997-2003.
Solid blocker.

84. Shannon Sharpe. TE, 1992-2003.
Super Bowl, two teams.

83. Wade Manning. WO, 1981-1982.
Lots of speed.

82. Vance Johnson. WO, 1985-1995.
One of the Three Amigos.

81. Steve Watson. WO, 1979-1987.
"The Blade," the long strider.

80. Rod Smith. WO, 1995-2005.
What a great free agent.

79. Barney Chavous. DL, 1973-1985.
Played the run great.

78. Matt Lepsis. OL, 1998-2005.
Protected the blind side.

77. Karl Mecklenburg. LB, 1983-1994.
Never took a play off.

76. Ken Lanier. OL, 1981-1992.

Thirteen years battling those big uglies.

75. Rulon Jones. DL, 1980-1985.
Sic 'em.

74. Mike Current. OL, 1967-1975.
Good upper body strength.

73. Simon Fletcher. DL, 1985-1995.
Sack master.

72. Keith Kartz. OL, 1987-1994.
Alex Gibbs groomed him.

71. Greg Kragen. DL, 1985-1993.
Cut early, then the Pro Bowl.

70. Paul Smith. DL, 1968-1978.
Ring of Fame.

69. Mark Schlereth. OL, 1995-2000.
Detective Roc Hoover on the Guiding Light soap opera.

68. Ruben Carter. DL, 1975-1986.
If you play 3-4 you need a nose guard.

67. George Goeddeke. OL, 1967-1972.
Dependable.

66. Tom Nalen. OL, 1994-2006.
Coach Shanahan called him "best ever."

65. Gary Zimmerman. OL, 1993-1997.
Should be in the Hall of Fame.

64. Bud McFaden. DL, 1960-1963.
Finished it up here.

63. Dave Costa. DL, 1967-1971.
Played in AFC and NFC.

62. Dan Neil. OL, 1997-2004.
Dependable Texan.

61. Andre Townsend. DL, 1984-1990.
Solid contribution.

60. Paul Howard. DL, 1976-1986.
Took Mean Joe's best punch.

59. Larry Kaminski. OL, 1966-1967.
Putts solid, before Nalen.

58. Steve Busick. LB, 1981-1985.
He and Dennison took on guards.

57. Tom Jackson. LB, 1973-1986.
Spirit, fire, hustle.

56. Al Wilson. LB, 1999-2005.
Was great in the locker room.

55. Pete Duranko. DE, 1967-1974.
Notre Dame guy was tough.

54. Keith Bishop. OL, 1980-1989.
On The Drive: "We got 'em right where we want 'em."

53. Bill Romanowski. LB, 1996-2001.
As intense as anyone.

52. Randy Gradishar. LB, 1974–1985.
In the Hall of Fame.

51. Bob Swenson. LB, 1975–1983.
Free agent could play.

50. Jim Ryan. LB, 1979–1988.
Guy from William and Mary, now coaches.

49. Dennis Smith. DB, 1981–1994.
He'd knock your head off.

48. Mike Leach. Long snapper, 2002.
Has never had a bad one.

47. John Lynch. DB, 2004–2006.
Wish we had him longer.

46. Dave Preston. RB, 1978–1983.
The Sarge ran hard.

45. Steve Wilson. DB, 1982–1988.
Stuck around a long time.

44. Floyd Little. RB, 1967–1975.
Saban once fired him.

43. Steve Foley. DB, 1976–1986.
Made the move from corner to safety.

42. Billy Van Heusen. WO, 1968–1976.
Steady in all phases.

41. Rob Lytle. RB, 1977–1983.
Never took a play off.

40. Charlie West. DB, 1978–1979.
Went on to coach.

39. Ray Crockett. LB, 1994–2000.
Good tackler.

38. Mike Anderson. RB, 2000–2005.
Great two years.

37. Cecil Sapp. RB, 2003–2005.
Can play fullback too.

36. Billy Thompson. DB, 1969–1981.
As good as we've ever had.

35. Larry Canada. FB, 1978-1991.
Impressive blocker.

34. Tyrone Braxton. DB, 1987-1999.
Chicken, great overachiever.

33. Jimmy Spencer. DB, 2000-2003.
He can coach too.

32. Jon Keyworth. RB, 1974-1980.
"Make Those Miracles Happen."

31. Mike Harden. DB, 1980-1988.
Solid cover and tackle.

30. Terrell Davis. RB, 1995-2001.
Best ever here.

29. Bernard Jackson. DB, 1977-1980.
Valuable member of Orange Crush.

28. Gaston Green. RB, 1991-1992.
Fastest ever?

27. Steve Atwater. DB, 1989-1998.
Remember the hit on Akoye?

26. Bobby Humphrey. RB, 1989-1991.
Had his moments.

25. Haven Moses. WO, 1972-1981.
M&M Connection.

24. Champ Bailey. DB, 2004-present.
Future Hall of Famer.

23. Austin "Goose" Gonsoulin. S, 1960-1966.
Ring of Fame.

22. Fran Lynch. RB, 1967-1976.
Solid when he got to play.

21. Gene Mingo. HBK, 1960-1964.
First punt return for a touchdown in the AFL.

20. Louis Wright. CB, 1975-1986.
Covered as good as Champ.

19. Fred Steinfort. Kicker, 1979-81.
Strong leg.

18. Frank Tripucka. QB, 1960-63.
Ring of Fame.

17. Steve Deberg. QB, 1981-83.
Kept the seat warm until Elway was ready.

16. Jake Plummer. QB, 2003-05.
Nobody had his arm strength rolling left.

15. Jim Turner. K, 1971-79.
I'll never forget his T.D. catch.

14. Brian Griese. QB, 1996-2002.
Coach Shanahan thought he could be another Montana.

13. Steve Tensi. QB, 1967-1970.
At times he looked good.

12. Charlie Johnson. QB, 1972-1975.
He was supposed to be washed up, he had something left.

11. Bobby Anderson. RB, 1970-73.
What if he hadn't got hurt?

10. Steve Ramsey. QB, 1971-1976.
For five years he was a pretty solid QB. Runner-up is Todd Sauerbrun if he doesn't punt to Devin Hester.

9. David Treadwell. Kicker, 1989-1992.
The guy from Clemson was clutch.

8. Gary Kubiak. QB, 1983-1991.
The coach for Houston was a reliable backup for Elway.

7. John Elway. QB, 1983-1998.
Hall of Famer. The runner-up wasn't bad: Craig Morton.

6. Bubby Brister. QB, 1997-1999.
He won some big games when Elway was injured.

5. Brad Daluiso. Kicker, 1992.
The only one who ever wore the number.

4. Chris Norman. Punter, 1986.
Remember the exhibition game when he was going to have to play quarterback?

3. Rich Karlis. Kicker, 1982-1988.
The barefoot kicker who was part of the famous drive.

2. Cookie Gilchrist. Fullback, 1965.

Might be the toughest to ever wear a Bronco uniform. Never played college ball.

1.Jason Elam. Kicker, 1993–2008.

He's a true superstar. Made a ton of clutch kicks.

O. Johnny Olszewski. RB, 1962.

Johnny O. played one year, 1962. He was better in college.

Try running through the alphabet, naming a Colorado sports legend for each letter. You might do better than we did. We think we did pretty well. Some names were called up from obscure depths of memory. The letter X presents a challenge.

Z. Zaharias.

Mildred "Babe" Didrikson Zaharias was perhaps the greatest female athlete ever in the U.S. She won two Olympic golds in track in 1932. Played champion golf and later became LPGA president. Her husband, George Zaharias, was a pro wrestler and promoter in Denver for a time. He was born in Pueblo, Colorado, but they called him "The Crying Greek for Cripple Creek."

Y. Starr Yelland.

The TV sportscaster who owned the market in the 1970s. A lot of people forget that he was a play-by-play announcer for Bears baseball. An outstanding broadcaster. A class act. Yelland was inducted into the Colorado Sports Hall of Fame in 2008.

X. Colorado Xplosion.

X is a tough letter. The Colorado Xplosion was the first women's pro basketball franchise in Colorado. It was a short-lived ABL team (not WNBA) from 1996 to 98.

W. Al Wilson.

Had great years as the Bronco middle linebacker.

V. Kiki Vandeweghe.

Greatest first step player for the Denver Nuggets. Became the General Manager.

U. Ted Uhlander.

Star outfielder for the Denver Bears. Had a solid Big League career for Minnesota. Nowadays he's a scout. Or Bobby Unser.

T. Roland "Fatty" Taylor.

He was anything but fat. Played solid defense for the Nuggets, 1974-75.

S. Freddy Joe Steinmark.

Star athlete at Wheat Ridge who played at Texas. Died of cancer at the age of 23, and is still a legend in Austin.

R. Greg Riddoch and Tom Runnels.

Greeley, Colorado, a town of 100,000, produced these two Major League Baseball managers, at San Diego and Montreal respectively.

Q. Jamie Quirk.

Rockies Bench Coach. Not only did he play pro baseball for seven Big League teams, he was a star quarterback in high school.

P. Scott Parker.

Avs Enforcer.

O. Johnny Olszewski.
Johnny "0." Wore number 0. Starred at Cal. Played for the Broncos in 1962.

N. Tom Nalen.
Broncos Center from Boston College. Been around since 1994. As good an offensive lineman as any in this program.

M. Billy Martin.
Played baseball Camp Carlson and managed the Denver Bears.

L. Dean Lahr.
The greatest wrestler to come out of this state. 1963-64 NCAA champion at CU, voted the MVP nationally in 1964.

K. Roger Kinney.
One of the real movers in this city. Brought the Final Four to Denver.

J. Bob Jeangerard.
Star Forward from CU who led Luckett Nix to the finals of the AAU Tournament. On the basketball team that won Olympic gold in 1956.

I. Hale Irwin.
The best golfer ever from Colorado. He was also All Big Eight as a safety in football.

H. Carroll Hardy.
The best all-around athlete at CU. Played pro football and pro baseball. Famous for pinch-hitting for Ted Williams.

G. Goose & Groove.
Gossage and Baylor. Enough said.

F. Frank Filchock.
The very first Denver Broncos coach. After he got fired he coached St. Joe's.

E. John Elway.
In addition to being a Hall of Fame quarterback and the most recognizable person in Colorado, he's a successful restaurateur.

D. Marvin Davis.
Denver Billionaire who had a handshake deal with Charles O. Finley to buy the Oakland A's. The deal was close and Al Rosen was going to be the General Manager. Didn't happen. Not that we're still bitter.

C. Jack Christiansen.
CSU great who was all pro with Detroit. Later coached Stanford.

B. Bus.

Bus Campbell. The pitching guru who worked with about 60 Big Leaguers. Passed away in 2008.

A. Michael Adams.

The little Denver Nugget who thrilled fans with his 3-pointers.

Our Namedropping List

We're proud to have talked with thousands of local and national sports figures on our show over the years. Here's a list of some of our notable guests. Let the namedropping begin.

Bob Knight.
The General. Say what you want, he's the winningest coach in NCAA Division 1 men's basketball.

John Wooden.
The Wizard of Westwood. Won 10 national championships coaching UCLA.

Bert Sugar.
The cigar-chomping, Runyonesque boxing writer.

Oscar De La Hoya.
The Golden Boy. Won Olympic gold for the U.S. boxing in Barcelona.

Bob Lilly.
Of Cowboys fame. Maybe the best defensive lineman ever.

Jim Valvano.
Coach Jimmy V, most notably of NC State University. Never give up.

Greg Gumbel.
The famous sportscaster.

Mike Krzyzewski.
Coach of the Duke Blue Devils.

Michael Jordan.
If you don't know, we can't help you.

Mickey Mantle.
One of the all-time greats. 1964 World Series walk-off homer. We remember it like yesterday.

Smokey Robinson.
When Smokey sings . . . we forget everything.

Whizzer White.
To you, it's Byron Raymond White, Supreme Court Justice.

Barry Switzer.
Coached at the University of Oklahoma and the Dallas Cowboys.

Bud Wilkinson.
Coached at Oklahoma. Posted a record 47-game winning streak from 1953-57.

Ralph Sampson.
Golden State Warrior and NBA star. Stood 7 feet 4 inches tall.

Bobby Bowden.
Head football coach of the Florida State Seminoles.

Steve Spurrier.
Won the Heisman Trophy in 1966. Coaches University of South Carolina football.

Bill McCartney.
Outstanding coach of CU Buffs football. Founded the Promise Keepers.

Lou Holtz.
One of the best and most beloved football coaches.

Bob Stoops.
Coached Oklahoma to an Orange Bowl win.

Larry Holmes.
Heavyweight boxing champ

Earnie Shavers.
Hard-punching heavyweight boxer.

Floyd Patterson.
We've had a ton of heavyweights on our show.

Jake LaMotta.
Raging Bull.

Archie Moore.
The Old Mongoose. Most knockouts of any fighter.

Tommy Hearns.
"Hit Man" welterweight.

Eddie Futch.
He trained champion fighters like Joe Frazier.

Mohammed Ali.
The Greatest.

John Madden and Al Michaels.
Monday nighters.

Brent Musberger.
Veteran sportscaster.

Vin Scully.
Play-by-play voice of the Dodgers.

Mario Lemieux.
Super Mario. Hockey great.

Stan Musial.
Stan the Man. One of the greatest baseball players of all time.

Warren Spahn.
Great lefty pitcher.

Billy Martin.
Most famous for managing the Yankees.

Don Larsen.
Pitched a perfect game in the 1956 World Series.

Gordie Howe.
A Detroit Red Wing that even Avalanche fans can love.

David Halberstam.
Pulitzer Prize-winning journalist.

Tom Lasorda.
Best known for managing the Dodgers.

Note: Vito "Babe" Parilli was a Broncos assistant coach from 1977 to 1999. He played for Bear Bryant at Kentucky, then for the Packers and the Cleveland Browns. He was one of the most productive quarterbacks in the AFL, playing for the Oakland Raiders, Boston Patriots and New York Jets. You might remember that he was Joe Namath's backup quarterback in Super Bowl III. In 1964, Parilli racked up almost 3,500 yards passing, mostly to Gino Cappelletti (who was also a place-kicker.) Parilli's nickname was "goldfinger" because he was among the best holders in pro football, holding for record-breaking kicker Jim Turner as well as Cappalletti. Most people don't know that Babe had a chance to play pro baseball. He was a solid shortstop. We asked Babe to list the nastiest defensive lineman he played against:

5. Earl Faison.
Always put steady pressure on you.

4. Ben Davidson.
Always tried to take your head off.

3. Doug Atkins.
Always tied up two blockers.

2. Lenny Ford.
Had a great get-off.

1. Gino Marchetti.
Fought in the battle of the bulge at age 17. He put Babe out of action for six weeks.

Worst Time Ever for Denver Sports

Remember the dark days of April and May, 2008? Here's a list of some of the bad news for Denver sports fans during that time.

6. The Crush and the Rapids.

Both teams have losing seasons.

5. The Mammoth.

Eliminated from the playoffs.

4. The Nuggets.

Swept from the first round of the playoffs. Haven't won a playoff series since 1994. Star Carmelo Anthony was arrested on drunken driving charges. Morale was at an all-time low.

3. The Avalanche.

Made it to the second round of the NHL playoff, but fell to the Red Wings. Forsberg and Foote were injured. There was talk that Sakic might end his career. "Coach Q" Joel Quenneville unceremoniously got the axe.

2. The Rockies.

In a severe slump. No sign of the previous season's Rocktober miracle. Top players, including Tulo, on the DL. Painful. Just painful.

1. The Broncos.

Jason Elam gone. Jay Cutler diagnosed with diabetes. Less-than-stellar draft picks. Ouch.

Irv Remembers When Softball Was King

Softball was king in Denver after World War II. Eddie Bohn's Pig and Whistle sponsored winter-league softball every Sunday, followed by a red-hot craps game. Softball games would draw huge crowds at City Park. These guys could bring it. No slow pitch here. It was dominated by pitching. Here are some of the very best players.

Jim Sparkman.
Firefighter. Had a great drop.

Eddie Bezjack.
A windmiller with a great change.

Audie Osborne.
A sweet-swinging left-handed hitter with power. His swing was classic. His son Danny was a pretty good pitcher who had a cup of coffee in the Big Leagues.

Allan "The Horse" Hower.
A left-handed hitting catcher with power. The Horse was also a good college basketball player at Regis.

Don Teske.
A gritty second-baseman who played at West High School. Teske was a left-handed hitter who always made contact.

Ray Weimar.
A sidewinder on the mound. His pitch was borderline illegal. Nobody threw harder.

Harvey Sterkle.
An 18-year-old from North High School, he was un-hittable. Eventually went to Chicago and pitched for the Aurora Sealmasters and was always a factor at national tournaments.

Pitcher Larry Bollig.
He's in the Colorado Sports Hall of Fame. A farm boy from Platteville, strong as an ox, could throw everyday. His business partner and teammate Dutch Hanel was a pretty fair infielder.

Two of the great hitters:
Jim Bolden and Art Unger.

Some other players worth mentioning:
Spider Over, Bill Moriarty, Pug Johnson, Fats Richardson, Sammy Levine, Gil Montoya, John Barnes.

Denver's favorite quarterback was inducted into the NFL Hall of Fame in 2004. Denver fans feel deep loyalty to John Elway. He played his entire career with the Broncos. He started in five Super Bowls, winning two back-to-back. He won 148 games in his pro career. He's the only player in NFL history to pass for 3,000 yards and rush for 200 yards in the same season seven consecutive times. He's one of the best ever. Elway also has an amazing 47 fourth-quarter or overtime game-winning or game-tying drives to his credit. All of them were significant. Here are a few of our favorite Elway comebacks.

7. December 11, 1983.
Elway comes alive against Balitmore in the fourth quarter, throwing three TDs for a 21 to 19 Denver win.

6. January 7, 1990.
Drives 71 yards for a TD to gain a one-point lead over Pittsburgh with under three minutes on the clock. Broncos win 24 to 23.

5. January 4, 1993.
Drives 87 yards in 12 plays for a field goal with 20 seconds on the clock. Broncos beat Houston 26 to 24.

4. January 17, 1988.
Executes five plays for 75 yards and a TD with four minutes on the clock. Broncos beat Cleveland 38 to 33.

3. January 4, 1998.
Against Kansas City in the AFC playoffs. Elway drives 49 yards in six plays. Terrell Davis punches across the goal line. Broncos win 14 to 10.

2. January 25, 1998.
Super Bowl against Green Bay. Elway directs five plays for 49 yards. Terrell Davis runs in a TD with less than two minutes on the clock. Broncos win it, 31-24.

1. January 11, 1987.
The Drive. Absolutely legendary.